Creatively Vegetarian

Creatively Vegetarian

A cookbook for vegetarians.

Recipes created and altered for the single vegetarian, using whole food, easily obtained, and low cost ingredients.

Meals are low fat or fat free and many are gluten free.

Salads

Cucumber Tomato Salad

 Cucumbers are prolific producers and this is a good way to use them. The dressing adds a nice tang!

Ingredients:
1 cup sliced cucumber
1/2 cup diced tomato
1/2 cup sliced celery
Parsley to taste
1 ounce firm tofu
1/2 tsp oil of choice
1 tsp lime juice
Salt
Pepper

Directions:
Mix the tofu, oil, lime juice, salt, and pepper until it makes a thick dressing, add water if necessary. Mix the vegetables and add the dressing. Stir well. Top with the fresh parsley.

Beet Bruschetta with Tofu and Basil

This was incredibly easy to make, beautiful to look at, and tasty to eat!

Ingredients:
1/2 cup diced beets
1 ounce firm tofu, cubed
2 basil leaves
Toasted bread of choice

Directions:
Boil the beets before dicing until just soft and rub the skins off.

Mix the tofu and beets. Spoon the mix onto the bread. Top with basil leaves. Serve!

Tomato, Beet, Tofu Salad

Not only is this delicious, it's very pretty!

Ingredients:
1/2 cup sliced tomato
1/2 cup sliced beets
1 ounce firm tofu, sliced
1 Tbsp fresh basil, shredded
1 Tbsp fresh parsley, shredded

Directions:
Mix all ingredients and serve!

Beet Radish Salad

I had radishes and pea pods from the garden and I thought they may taste good with the beets I'd just harvested. I was right! This is a great combination.

Ingredients:
1/2 cup diced beet
1/2 cup pea pods
1/2 cup corn
1/2 cup diced radish
1/4 cup quinoa
1 ounce firm tofu, diced

Directions:
Boil the beet root prior to making this. As the beet gets just soft, remove it and rub the skin off.

Warm the quinoa and corn for about 30 seconds in the microwave. Mix in with the remaining ingredients. Salt and pepper to taste.

Radish Cucumber Salad

This is a nice, cool dish for summer. A perfect way to use that garden produce. Mine is made with radishes and cucumber from the community garden and peas from my backyard garden.

Ingredients:
3/4 cup diced radish
3/4 cup diced cucumber
1/2 cup peas or pea pods
1/4 cup cooked quinoa
1 ounce firm tofu
1/4 tsp red wine vinegar
Salt
Pepper

Directions:
Crush the tofu in enough water to make a thick sauce and add the red wine vinegar. Mix all ingredients together and add the tofu sauce. Salt and pepper to taste.

Dutch Lettuce

This particular recipe is a family adaptation of a dish that came with my relatives from Belgium.

Ingredients:
1 egg hard boiled
1/2 cup diced cooked potato
1 cup greens
1 ounce firm tofu
Salt
Pepper

Directions:
Using water, make a gravy out of the tofu, salt, and pepper. I like cracked black pepper for this. Spread the greens on a plate. Add the potato. Chop the egg and add. Then, warm the tofu gravy and pour that over the whole dish. Serve!

Southwestern Barley Salad

 I cooked my barley earlier in the week, so this was very simple to toss together. It didn't, however, take long to cook a 1/4 cup of barley. It's only a tablespoon of the dried variety!

Ingredients:
1/4 cup cooked barley
1/2 cup corn
1/2 cup diced tomato
1/4 cup cooked black beans
1 tsp lime juice
Salt
Pepper

Directions:
Heat the barley and beans in the microwave. Mix in the remaining ingredients. Serve.

White Bean Medley

The combination of cumin and basil is really quite tasty.

Ingredients:
1/2 cup white beans
1/2 cup sliced zucchini
1/2 cup sliced carrots
1/2 cup sliced summer squash
1/2 cup sliced mushrooms
1/4 teaspoon cumin
Two basil leaves crushed

Directions:
Heat the beans in the microwave until warm. Mix in with the rest of the ingredients, including the spices. Serve.

Roasted Potato Salad

Try this dish on an evening when there's a bit of a chill so you don't heat up the kitchen baking the potato!

Ingredients:
1/2 cup cubed potato
1/2 cup pea pods
1 cup mixed greens
1/2 tsp rosemary
Salt
Pepper

Directions:
Mix the potatoes with rosemary, salt, and pepper. Bake at 350 until tender, about 20 minutes. Toss the greens on a plate, put the pea pods on the greens, then put the potatoes on top. Serve!

Quinoa Mexican Salad

A great way to enjoy those garden greens in a Mexican dish.

Ingredients:
1/4 cup quinoa
1/4 cup cooked beans
1 ounce cubed firm tofu
1/2 cup diced tomatoes
1/2 cup corn
1/4 cup chopped red pepper
3/4 cup greens
1/4 teaspoon cumin
1/4 teaspoon paprika
Salt

Directions:
Heat quinoa and beans in the microwave. Add the spices and all other ingredients except the greens and mix well. Spread the greens on a plate and top with the mixture. Serve.

Carrots and Peas

Ginger is pretty hot. If you don't like too much spice, you'll want to reduce the amount in this recipe. I set my mouth on fire!

Ingredients:
1/2 cup grated carrots
1/2 cup pea pods
1 ounce firm tofu
1/4 tsp ginger
1/2 tsp cinnamon
Salt

Directions:
Toss carrots, tofu,
and pea pods with the spices and serve.

Dilled Corn and Pea Pods

This was made with fresh pea pods and fresh dill from my garden! I do adore summer. However, it could be done with dried dill and pea pods from other people's gardens and taste just as good.

Ingredients:
1/2 cup corn
1/4 cup pea pods, trimmed
1 ounce tofu
3 sprigs fresh dill or 1 tsp dried

Directions:
Mix the dill, tofu, and a bit of water to make a thick sauce. Mix the corn and pea pods and toss with the sauce. Serve and eat!

Corn Tomato Basil Salad

Hot summer night? No need to heat up the kitchen, throw this together for a delicious meal.

Ingredients:
1/2 cup corn
1/2 cup diced tomato
1 ounce firm tofu cubed
3 leaves fresh basil

Directions:
Mix the ingredients. Cut the basil into the mixture.   Serve over greens.

Fresh Veggies and Quinoa

A good deal of prep work with all the slicing and dicing, but well worth it!

Ingredients:
1/4 cup cooked quinoa
1/4 cup diced carrot
1/4 cup chopped celery
1/4 cup diced zucchini
1/4 cup diced yellow squash
1/4 cup chopped radish
1/4 cup diced parsnip
1/4 cup chopped mushroom
1/4 cup diced tomato
1 ounce firm tofu cubed
Salt
Pepper

Directions:
Warm quinoa. Mix all ingredients. Eat!

Greek Salad

I have to say, this was quite good. Plus, the added bonus of not heating up the kitchen on a hot day!

Ingredients:
1/2 cup sliced mushrooms
1/2 cup diced tomato
1/2 cup cooked white beans
1/4 tsp oregano
Salt
Pepper

Directions:
Heat the beans. Mix all ingredients. Eat!

Pea and Radish Salad

I used frozen peas for this, but I'm looking forward to trying it with fresh peas or maybe even pea pods!

Ingredients:
1 cup mixed greens
1/2 cup peas
1/2 cup diced radish
1 tsp lemon juice
1 tsp red wine vinegar
1/2 tsp oil
Salt
Pepper

Directions:
Mix and eat!

Beet and Split Pea Salad

You could use fresh beets, canned beets, or pickled beets in this recipe. I used pickled beets because I'm fond of the tangy flavor!

Ingredients:
1 cup cooked split peas
1/2 cup diced beets
1/2 cup leafy greens
1 ounce firm tofu
1 tsp basil
Salt
Pepper

Directions:
Mix and eat!

"Tuna" Salad Sandwich

Easy, filling, and no heating up the kitchen!

Ingredients:
1/2 cup cooked white beans
1/2 cup celery
1 tsp dill
Salt
Pepper

Directions:
Purée the beans. Mix in celery, dill, salt, and pepper. Spread on bread.

Mock Tuna Salad

A great dish for a warm summer evening!   Yogurt could be substituted for the tofu, if you prefer. I would use 1/4 cup.

Ingredients:
1/2 cup sliced celery
1/2 cup diced carrot
1/2 cup peas
1/2 cup diced tomato
1 oz tofu
1 tsp dill
Salt
Pepper

Directions:
If your tofu is firm, add water and mix until you have a smooth sauce. Add the dill, salt to taste, and black pepper to taste. Mix the vegetables together, add the dill sauce and combine well.

Wraps

White Bean Artichoke Basil Wrap

This includes a lot of filling, you may desire two tortillas for two wraps! Or, you could put the rest of the filling on the side.

Ingredients;
1/2 cup artichoke hearts
1 cup mixed greens
2 Tbsp fresh basil
1/2 cup cooked white beans
1 tsp lemon juice
Salt
Pepper
1 tortilla

Directions:
Purée beans, 1 Tbsp basil, lemon juice, salt, and pepper. Chop the rest of the basil and mix it in. Spread this on the tortilla. Top with the greens and artichoke hearts and roll it up.

Microwave

Mexican Split Peas

I prepared my split peas earlier in the week, so this was quite quick to throw together.

Ingredients:
1 cup cooked split peas
1/2 cup diced tomato
1/4 cup corn
1/4 cup sliced and quartered zucchini
1/4 cup black beans
1 ounce firm tofu, cubed
1/4 cup rice or quinoa
1/4 tsp cumin
1/4 tsp paprika
dash cayenne
salt

Directions:
Mix all the ingredients and heat through, about 2 minutes in the microwave.

Butternut Sketti

Squash with cinnamon and salt is just the tastiest dish ever!

Ingredients:
1 cup cooked spaghetti squash
1/2 cup cubed cooked butternut squash
1/2 cup sweet corn
1/4 tsp cinnamon
Salt

Directions:
Mix the ingredients in a bowl and microwave until heated through, about two minutes. Serve.

Quinoa Tacos

You'll notice in the photo that I mixed my quinoa with some rice. I took the photo so you could see the consistency of the mixture!

Ingredients:
1/4 cup cooked quinoa
1/4 tsp cumin
1/4 tsp paprika
2 tsp water
Tortilla

Directions:
Mix the quinoa, water, and spices. You want a clumpy mixture so add more water if necessary. Salt to taste. Spoon into the tortilla and top off with garnishes you choose!

Corn, Tomato, Black Bean, Quinoa Mixer

You could do this with rice, barley, or any similar grain/seed.

Ingredients:
1/2 cup corn
1/2 cup black beans
1/2 cup diced tomato
1/4 cup quinoa
1/4 tsp cumin
1/4 tsp paprika
Salt

Directions:
Mix all ingredients in a microwave safe bowl and heat about a minute and thirty seconds. Serve!

Black Bean Quinoa

The spice in this is HOT. I suggest testing as you add. The smoky flavor, though, really "makes" this dish!

Ingredients:
1/2 cup cooked black beans
1/4 cup chopped red pepper
1/4 cup cooked quinoa
1/8 tsp chipotle chile spice
Salt
Pepper

Directions:
Mix the ingredients and heat in the microwave until warm. Serve!

Zucchini Caulifredo

I do not have a spiralizer. However, fettucini noodles are wider so I thought a carrot peeler would work. It works wonderfully well! I actually froze the rest of this zucchini to make vegetable broth on another day.

Ingredients:
1/2 cup cooked white beans
1/2 cup cooked cauliflower
1 cup zucchini noodles
Salt
Pepper

Directions:
Use a carrot peeler to make broad zucchini "noodles."
Put the beans and cauliflower and a 1/2 tsp of your oil of choice in a food processor or blender and whir smooth. Mix with the noodles and use salt and pepper to taste. Heat in the microwave until warmed through. Serve!

Corny Sketti

Sweet corn is fresh from the fields! I used the last of my frozen spaghetti squash for this one and it was so worth it.

Ingredients:
1 cup cooked spaghetti squash
1 cup sweet corn off the cob
1 ounce firm tofu cubed
Salt

Directions:
Mix the squash, tofu, and the corn and warm in the microwave for about a minute and thirty seconds. Salt it to taste. If you want, add a little real butter or olive oil to bring out even more flavor from the corn.

Judara

This is traditionally made with lentils and rice. I cooked the split peas and quinoa in advance so I could just toss this together on a hot evening without heating up the kitchen.

Ingredients:
3/4 cooked split peas
1/4 cup cooked quinoa
1/2 cup sliced and quartered cucumber
1/2 cup diced tomato
1 ounce firm tofu
1 tablespoon lemon juice
2 Tbsp chopped fresh parsley
Salt

Directions:
Warm the peas and quinoa. Place peas and quinoa on a plate. Mix the cucumber, tomato, parsley, lemon juice, and salt. Put this mixture on top of the peas and quinoa. Eat!

Zucchini Sketti

I purchase and cook spaghetti squash early in the season, then I freeze it to enjoy in the off-season. Because of that, this dish is a quick throw together!

Ingredients:
1/2 cup diced zucchini
1/4 cup diced mushrooms
1 cup cooked spaghetti squash
1/4 cup tomato sauce
Salt
Pepper

Directions:
Mix ingredients. Heat in the microwave. Serve and eat!!

Tofu and White Bean Salad

A meal for a hot summer evening. Little preparation required for a superb taste.

Ingredients:
1oz tofu
1/4 cup cooked white beans
1/4 cup wax beans
1/4 cup green beans
1/4 cup corn
1/4 cup peas
1 tsp red wine vinegar
1 tsp parsley
Salt
Pepper

Directions:
Combine the ingredients and heat in the microwave. Serve over greens, quinoa, or pasta.

Sweet Potato Black Bean Burrito

These flavors combine beautifully in a burrito.

Ingredients:
1/2 cup cubed cooked sweet potato
1/2 cup cooked black beans
Tortilla

Directions:
Mix and heat. Whir until smooth in a food processor or blender or squish with a fork. Spread on the tortilla and roll it up. Serve with Rotel, tomatoes, shredded lettuce, cheese, sour cream, guacamole....the possibilities are endless!

Spinach Sketti

Really a nice combination and very easy to prepare.

Ingredients:
1 cup spaghetti squash
1/2 cup cooked spinach
1/4 cup diced tomato
1/4 cup chopped mushroom
1/2 tsp basil
1/2 tsp parsley
Salt
Pepper

Directions:
Mix and heat!

Artichoke Sketti

I do like my spaghetti squash!

Ingredients:
1 cup cooked spaghetti squash
1/2 cup artichoke hearts
1/4 cup diced tomato
1/4 cup chopped mushroom
Salt
Pepper

Directions:
Mix and heat and eat.

Basil Sketti

Utterly delightful!

Ingredients:
1 cup spaghetti squash, cooked
1/4 cup noodles
1/2 cup chopped mushroom
1/2 cup diced tomato
1 Tbsp fresh, crushed basil
1/2 tsp oil

Directions:
Mix all ingredients and heat through. Add salt if desired.

Spring Rolls

Now, one of these ingredients does not follow my easy procurement

My seaweed "chips" come to me through my sister who is in a bigger city in another state. But, they are delicious...so....

Ingredients:

1.5 cup carrots, radishes, celery, zucchini, mushrooms.
1/4 cup quinoa
1oz firm tofu
1/2 tsp oil
1/2 tsp red wine vinegar
Salt
Pepper

Seaweed or nuri wraps of choice.

Directions:

I put all ingredients in the food processor and whirred it until it was of a grainy consistency. Warm up the mix. Then, put spoonfuls in your wraps and roll them up. My seaweed is small rectangles, so I didn't cut them coin sized.

"Lobster" Salad

First, I should share that I have a food sensitivity to sulfite. Thus, all foods containing sulfite are something I avoid...especially if they are high in that fun little friend. These foods are definitely garlic, onion, leek, scallion, green pepper, lentil, broccoli, cauliflower, beer, and wine. You'll find none of my recipes contain these ingredients. Feel free to add them to yours, that's the whole point of creatively cooking - go ahead, step out of the recipe box!

I've altered this recipe so much that the original creator likely wouldn't recognize it. I removed the scallions, for one, due to that pesky sulfite sensitivity and the fact my grocery store doesn't have them. I also used button mushrooms, those nice white ones you can find in any grocery store. The original called for Lion's Mane mushrooms. This would probably also lend itself well to baby 'bellas, if you can find them.

I did not cook my mushrooms first because, why waste all those fun nutrients by cooking them out? Of course, you could save the cook water as broth for later.

Ingredients:
1 cup chunked mushrooms (chunk them pretty large)
1/4 cup thin sliced celery
1/4 cup diced tomato
1/4 cup corn
1/4 cup diced carrots
Salt
Dash of Old Bay

Put all food ingredients in a bowl and mix. Add the salt. Then, add a dash of Old Bay. If you like foods spicy, you should add as much as you would like, but you don't want to overpower the flavors of the ingredients! Heat in the microwave for a minute, just until the mushrooms are a bit soft.

Serve over greens or on a rice cake like pictured! I also plated pinto beans and warmed, chunked tofu.

"Cheesy" Sketti

As a vegetarian, I often find recipes that others may find quirky. I mean, why not just use real cheese? I'm not a vegan, so.... But, as the blog title says, "Creatively Vegetarian." If I can create something similar using readily available items and it's not processed through a factory, I will!

This took a little experimentation to make it for a single portion. I hope you enjoy!

Ingredients:
1 cup cooked spaghetti squash
1/4 cup cooked pasta noodles
1/4 mushed up cooked butternut squash
1Tbsp + 1tsp Nutritional yeast
Salt
Water

Directions:
Add the nutritional yeast and salt to the mushed up squash. Add water until it's a consistency you want. I used this as a sauce for the "spaghetti" and I don't like my sauce too watery. Mix the sauce with the spaghetti squash and pasta and heat. Serve!

I plated mine with green beans frozen from the garden, pan toasted firm tofu, and mixed beans.

Butternut Squash Sketti

What a great way to combine some winter squashes!

Ingredients:
1 cup spaghetti squash
1/2 cup cooked butternut squash
1/4 cup chunked up seitan
1/2 cup tomato sauce
1/2 tsp basil (more to taste)
1/4 tsp sage (more to taste)
salt to taste

Directions:
Sautee the butternut squash and seitan with the basil and sage until the seitan has a bit of crunch. Mix with the spaghetti squash and tomato sauce (add more basil and sage if you desire). Heat in the microwave for approximately 2 minutes or until heated through.

For The Crock

Parsnip Soup

This brings the HEAT, so be prepared!

Ingredients:
1/2 cup sliced parsnip
1/2 tsp curry
1/2 cup water or vegetable broth
salt to taste

Directions:
 Place all ingredients in the baby crock for 4-6 hours or until the parsnip is tender.

Spinach Soup

Do not forget the "sauce" on top, it really sets this off nicely.

Ingredients:
1/2 cup cooked spinach
1/2 cup diced potato
1 Tbsp dried pinto beans
1/2 cup water
Salt
Pepper
1 ounce firm tofu (or 1 Tbsp yogurt)

Directions:
Place all the ingredients except the tofu in the baby crock on low for 4-6 hours. Mix the tofu with enough water to make a thick sauce. Before serving, top the soup with the tofu sauce.

Black Bean Soup with Cornbread Dumpling

The ultimate in tastiness! Even with the dumpling preparation, this only took about 10 minutes of work.

Ingredients:
2 Tbsp dried black beans
1/4 cup Rotel
1/4 cup diced tomato
1/2 cup water
1 bay leaf

Dumpling:
3 Tbsp cornmeal
1 Tbsp flour
1/2 tsp baking powder
pinch baking soda
pinch salt
1/2 tsp oil
1 Tbsp milk
1 Tbsp + 1tsp water

Directions:
Place the beans, Rotel, tomato, water, bay leaf, and salt to taste in the baby crock for 4 - 6 hours. Approximately 30 minutes before serving, mix the dumpling ingredients and spoon the mixture on top of the soup. Cover and let cook for 30 minutes. Serve!

Slow Cooker Burrito

This recipe makes enough for several burritos, or just eat the remainder as a side dish.

Ingredients:
2 Tbsp uncooked black beans
2 Tbsp uncooked rice
1/4 cup diced tomato
1/4 tsp cumin
1/4 tsp paprika
Salt to taste
1 cup water
Tortilla

Directions:
Place all ingredients except the tortilla into the baby crock. Cook on low for 4-6 hours or until the beans and rice are tender. Spread in the tortilla and serve.

Cauliflower Dumpling Soup

If you like your soup to have more "juice," you'll need to add more water. The dumpling sucks some up.

Ingredients:
1/2 cup cauliflower
1/4 cup corn
1/4 cup diced potato
1/2 cup water
Salt
Pepper

--Dumpling
1/4 cup flour
1/2 tsp baking powder
1/4 tsp baking soda
water to make thick dough

Directions:
Place the ingredients (not the dumpling) in the baby crock on low for 4-6 hours, until the potato is tender. 30 minutes before serving, mix the dumpling and spoon on top of the soup.

Sweet Potato Soup

I served this with tortilla chips and it was very tasty!

Ingredients:
1/2 cup diced sweet potato
1/2 cup corn
1/4 tsp cumin
1/4 tsp paprika
salt to taste
1/2 cup water
1 Tbsp Greek yogurt

Directions:
Put all the ingredients except the yogurt in the baby crock on low for 4-6 hours. Stir the soup until it's smooth and add the yogurt before serving.

Kapustnik Belorusskey

Do not forget to remove the bay leaf before eating!

Ingredients:
1/2 cup mushrooms
1/2 cup sauerkraut
1/2 cup sliced carrot
1/2 cup diced potato
1/4 tsp nutmeg
1/4 tsp caraway seeds
1/4 tsp paprika
1 bay leaf
Pepper
Salt

Directions:
Place all ingredients in the baby crock on low for 4-6 hours, until the carrots and potatoes are tender.

Tuscan Soup

I used kale I had frozen from the garden last fall. I think I would add more basil next time!

Ingredients:
2 Tbsp uncooked white beans
1/2 cup diced tomato
1 cup kale
1 tsp basil
1/2 cup water
Salt to taste

Directions:
Place all ingredients in the baby crock on low for 4-6 hours, or until the beans are tender.

Vegetarian Ribollita

I wasn't sure about the bread in this, but it's really good!

Ingredients:
1/4 cup sliced celery
1/4 cup sliced carrot
1/2 cup shredded cabbage
1/2 cup cooked spinach
1/4 cup sliced and quartered zucchini
1/4 cup diced tomato
2Tbsp dried white beans
1/4 tsp rosemary
1/4 tsp basil
1/4 tsp marjoram
1/2 cup water or veggie broth
1 slice of sourdough bread

Directions:
Place all ingredients except the bread into the baby crock for 4-6 hours, until the beans are tender. About 10 minutes before serving, cut the bread into small squares and put it in the crock.

Butternut Squash Soup Variant

The tomato really adds a nice tangy flavor to this soup.

Ingredients:
1 cup butternut squash
1/2 cup corn
1/4 cup diced tomato
2 Tbsp uncooked pinto beans
1/2 cup water
Salt to taste

Directions:
Put all the ingredients in the baby crock on low for 4-6 hours or until the beans are tender.

Berlin Kartoffelsuppe

I do like the caraway flavor!

Ingredients:
1/4 cup diced potato
1/2 cup sliced carrot
1/2 cup sliced celery
1/2 cup vegetable broth or water
1 tsp parsley
1 bay leaf
1/4 tsp marjoram
1/4 tsp caraway seeds
1/4 tsp nutmeg
Salt
Pepper

Directions:
Place all ingredients in the baby crock and cook on low for 4-6 hours. Remove the bay leaf before eating.

Kholodnik (Modified)

I will add more parsley and some pepper in the future.

Ingredients:

1/4 cup sweet potato, cubed
1/4 cup potato, cubed
1/2 cup diced beets
1/4 cup sliced zucchini
1/2 tsp parsley
1 tsp lemon juice
salt to taste
1/2 cup water or veggie broth

Directions:
Place all ingredients in the baby crock on low for 4-6 hours.

Tikel Gomen

An unusual dish with very simple preparation.

Ingredients:
1 cup cabbage, shredded
1/2 cup sliced carrot
1/2 cup diced potato
1 ounce firm tofu, cubed
1/2 tsp cumin
1/2 tsp turmeric
1/4 tsp ginger
1/2 cup water
salt
pepper

Directions:
Place all ingredients in the baby crock on low for 4-6 hours.

Taco Soup

I suggest eating this soup with tortilla chips!

Ingredients:
2 Tbsp dried kidney beans
1/2 cup diced tomato
1/4 cup corn
1/4 tsp cumin
1/4 tsp paprika
dash cayenne
1/2 cup water

Directions:
Place all ingredients in the baby crock for 4-6 hours.

Portobello Mushroom Pot Roast

I used "baby 'bellas" because that's what my grocery store had, but if you can find the big caps, try those!

Ingredients:
1 cup portobello mushrooms
1/4 cup sliced carrots
1/4 cup diced potato
1/4 tsp sage
1/4 tsp basil
1/4 tsp rosemary
salt
pepper
1/2 cup veggie broth or water

Directions:
Place all ingredients in the baby crock for 4-6 hours. Thicken the broth with arrowroot or cornstarch before serving.

Lobio Mtsuanilit (Herbed Kidney Beans)

This is the main protein dish for a meal, but you will need to add side dishes.

Ingredients:
2 Tbsp uncooked kidney beans
1/2 cup water
1 tsp red wine vinegar
1 tsp parsley
1 tsp dill
1 tsp basil

Directions:
Mix all the ingredients in the baby crock and turn on low for 4-6 hours, until the beans are tender.

Black Bean Soup

Super simple preparation and a great taste! I served this with tortilla chips.

Ingredients:
2Tbsp dried black beans
1/2 cup diced tomato
1/2 cup water
Salt

Directions:
Place the ingredients in the baby crock on low until the beans are tender, approximately 4-6 hours.

Irish Stew

You could thicken this with a bit of arrowroot or corn starch to make it a little more stew-like, but I found it quite good as is.

Ingredients:
1/4 cup carrot
1/4 cup turnip
1/4 cup potato
1/4 cup sweet potato
1/4 cup celery
1/4 cup parsnip
1/2 cup spinach
1Tbsp white beans
1/2 cup water or veggie broth
Parsley
Salt
Pepper

Directions:
Place all ingredients in the baby crock on low until the vegetables are tender, 4-6 hours.

Borscht

There are many recipes for this, I tweaked a couple together!

Ingredients:
1/2 cup sliced beets
1/2 cup diced potatoes
1/2 cup saurkraut
1/4 cup sliced carrot
1/4 cup tomato sauce
1 ounce firm tofu, cubed
salt and pepper to taste
1 tsp parsley
1 tsp dill

Directions:
Put all ingredients in the baby crock and cook on low for 4-6 hours (until the potatoes are tender).

Sauerkraut Soup

An interesting German soup.

Ingredients:
1/2 cup saurkraut
1/4 cup diced potato
1/4 cup sliced mushroom
1/4 cup diced carrot
1/4 cup sliced celery
1 tsp dill
Salt to taste
1/2 cup water

Directions:
Place all the ingredients in the baby crock on low for 4-6 hours. If you would like it more "soupy," add more water.

Greek Split Pea Soup

What a great way to change up a traditional split pea soup!

Ingredients:
1/3 cup dried split peas
1 ounce firm tofu, cubed
1/2 cup diced tomato
1/4 tsp sage
1/4 tsp rosemary
1/4 tsp majoram
1/4 tsp oregano
Salt to taste
3/4 cup water or veggie broth

Directions:
Put all ingredients in the baby crock on low for 4 -6 hours.

Squash Curry

You could substitute lentils for the split peas. I really enjoyed it with the split peas, though!

Ingredients:
1Tbsp uncooked pinto beans
2Tbsp + 2 tsp uncooked split peas
1/4 cup diced tomato
1/2 cup tomato sauce
1/4 cup cubed butternut squash
1/4 cup diced potato
1/4 cup sliced carrot
1/4 cup cooked spinach
1/2 tsp curry
1/4 tsp cumin
salt to taste
1/2 cup water

Directions:
Place all ingredients in the baby crock and cook on low for 4 - 6 hours.

Tomato Corn Soup

What an easy soup to prepare! The results are delicious!

Ingredients:
1 cup chopped tomato
1/2 cup corn
1 ounce firm tofu, cubed
1/4 cup water
Salt to taste

Directions:
Place all ingredients in the baby crock and cook on low for 4 - 6 hours.

Mushroom Barley Soup

For more of a mushroom flavor, leave out the rosemary and thyme.

Ingredients:
1Tbsp uncooked barley
1/2 cup sliced mushrooms
1/2 cup sliced carrots
1/2 cup sliced celery
1/4 tsp thyme
1/4 tsp rosemary
Parsley to taste
Salt to taste
3/4 cup water or veggie broth

Directions:
Put all the ingredients in the baby crock on low until the barley is tender, 4-6 hours.

Potato Dumpling Soup

Easy soup with a dumpling!

Ingredients:
1/4 cup flour
1/2 tsp baking powder
1/4 tsp baking soda
water

1/2 cup diced potato
1/4 cup corn
1/4 cup peas
1/2 cup water or veggie broth
Salt to taste

Directions:
Put the potato, corn, peas, water/broth, and salt in the baby crock on low for 4-6 hours. 30 minutes before you're ready to serve, mix up the dough for the dumpling. Add just enough water to make a very thick, sticky dough. Drop this dough on top of the soup and cover the crock pot for the last 30 minutes. Serve it up!

Roasted Tomato Soup

I used Roma tomatoes, but any variety will work.

Ingredients:
1 cup quartered tomatoes
1/4 tsp oregano
1/4 tsp basil
Salt
1/2 tsp oil
Water to thin the soup to your desired consistency

Directions:
Mix the tomatoes with the oil, oregano, and salt and spread on a baking sheet. Roast at 400 degrees for 15 minutes or until the tomatoes are soft. Put the tomatoes in a food processor or blender and add the basil. Whir until smooth. Pour into a bowl and serve.

Acorn Squash Soup

The carrot adds a touch of sweetness not to be missed.

Ingredients:
1 cup acorn squash cubed
1/4 cup chopped carrot
1/4 tsp sage
Salt
Pepper
1/2 cup water or veggie broth

Directions:
Place all ingredients in the baby crock on low for 4 to 6 hours. Serve!

Mushroom Goulash

Depending on how strongly you like your food flavored, you could reduce the amount of fennel seeds.

Ingredients:
1/2 cup sliced mushrooms
1/2 cup diced tomatoes
1/4 cup tomato sauce
1/4 cup veggie broth
1/4 tsp paprika
1/4 tsp oregano
1/4 tsp fennel seed

Directions:
Place all ingredients in the baby crock on low. Cook for 4-6 hours. Serve with noodles!

Tomato and Pinto Bean Soup

I expected this to taste like a thicker tomato soup, but it didn't at all! What a great nutty flavor!

Ingredients:
1 cup diced tomato
2 Tbsp dried pinto beans
1/2 cup water or veggie broth
Salt
Pepper

Directions:
Place ingredients in the baby crockpot. Salt and pepper to taste. Cook on low until the beans are tender. Whir in a food processor or blender until smooth. Serve.

Summer Veggie Stew

Throw it all in the crock and enjoy 4 hours later!

Ingredients:
1/2 cup cubed and peeled eggplant
1/2 cup green beans
1/4 cup sliced zucchini
1/4 cup sliced yellow squash
1/4 cup corn
1/4 cup diced tomato
1/2 tsp apple cider vinegar
1/4 tsp oregano
Salt
Pepper
1/2 cup water

Directions:
Place all ingredients in the baby crock and cook on low 4-6 hours.

Zucchini, Yellow Squash, Corn Soup

A great combination of garden vegetables!

Ingredients:
1/2 cup small cubed zucchini
1/2 cup small cubed yellow squash
1/2 cup corn
1/2 cup shredded kale
2 Tbsp dried white beans
Salt
Pepper
1/2 cup water or veggie broth

Directions:
Put all ingredients in the baby crock on low until the beans are tender, 4-6 hours.

Vegetarian Booyah

This is a traditional Belgian dish that I have taken a couple of liberties with. First, I made it vegetarian when it calls for both beef and chicken. Second, I've made it in a single portion when it is usually made in two to three large kettles meant to serve an entire community!

Ingredients:
1/4 cup cubed potato
1/4 cup corn
1/4 cup sliced carrot
1/2 cup green beans
1/4 cup diced tomato
1/4 cup sliced celery
1/4 cup kale
3/4 cup veggie broth
1/4 tsp basil
1/4 tsp oregano
1/4 tsp celery salt
Salt
Pepper

Directions:
Mix all ingredients in the baby crock. Cook on low until the potatoes are tender, 4-6 hours.

Corn Chowder #2

This version of corn chowder uses fresh sweet corn and includes the cob during cooking.

Ingredients:
1 medium ear of corn, cooked
1/4 cup chopped carrot
1/4 cup chopped celery
1/4 cup diced potato
1/4 cup chopped banana pepper
1/2 cup water or veggie broth
Salt
Pepper
1/4 tsp thyme
1 bay leaf

Directions:
Cut the corn off the cob. Place all ingredients, including the cob, in the baby crock on low for 4-6 hours. Remove the cob and bay leaf before eating.

Radish Soup

Corn and radish! What a great combination!

Ingredients:
1/2 cup corn
1/2 cup diced radish
1/2 cup sliced carrot
1/4 cup diced potato
1/2 cup veggie broth or water
Salt

Directions:
Place all ingredients in the baby crock on low until the vegetables are tender, about 5 hours.

Rhubarb Quinoa

A tangy treat for a warm summer evening! The rosemary "makes" this dish.

Ingredients:
1 cup rhubarb
1 1/2 Tbsp uncooked quinoa
1/2 cup water
1/2 tsp rosemary
Salt
Pepper

Directions:
Place all ingredients in the baby crock on low until the quinoa is tender, about 3 hours.

Rhubarb Split Pea Soup

 One of my objectives in making meals is to use produce that is local and in season. Rhubarb is in season now and I used some that came from my community garden...fresh as fresh can be!

Ingredients:
1/3 cup dried split peas
1/2 cup sliced rhubarb
1/4 cup sliced carrot
1/4 cup sliced celery
1 cup water
Salt
Pepper

Directions:
Put all ingredients in the baby crock in low until the peas are tender.

Rhubarb and Beet Soup

One could use fresh or canned beets in this. I used pickled beets and I highly recommend that approach! Nicely tangy.

Ingredients:
1/2 cup diced beets
1/2 cup diced rhubarb
1/2 cup chopped parsnip
1/4 cup chopped carrot
2/3 cup water
Salt

Directions:
Place all ingredients in the baby crock on low for 4-6 hours, until the parsnip and carrot are tender.

Potato, Bean, and Kale Soup

A nice meal for a warm day. Easy prep and no heating up the kitchen. Light fare!

Ingredients:
1 cup torn up kale
1/2 cup sliced carrot
1/2 cup cubed sweet potato
2Tbsp dried white beans
3/4 cup water or veggie broth
1/4 tsp oregano
1/4 tsp thyme
1/2 tsp parsley
Bay leaf
Salt
Pepper

Directions:
Put all ingredients in the baby crock on low until the veggies and beans are tender, 4-6 hours.

Two Bean Soup with Kale

An intriguing flavor to this soup. A nice way to use the kale that should be coming ready for harvest.

Ingredients:
1Tbsp dried white beans
1Tbsp dried pinto beans
1 cup shredded kale
1/2 cup chopped carrot
1/2 cup chopped celery
1/4 tsp Rosemary
1 tsp red wine vinegar
1/2 tsp oil
Salt
Pepper
1/2 cup veggie broth or water

Directions:
Put all ingredients in the baby crock on low until beans are tender. 4-6 hours.

Scottish Vegetable Soup

I used saurkraut in this recipe, but you could use cabbage. I also used sweet potato instead of white potato. So, there are some options for you to modify this to your tastes!

Ingredients:
1/4 cup chopped celery
1/2 cup sliced carrots
1/2 cup sliced parsnips
1/4 cup cubed sweet potato
1/4 cup shredded cabbage or saurkraut
1/4 cup chopped mushroom
1Tbsp uncooked barley
1/2 cup veggie broth or water
Salt to taste

Directions:
All ingredients go in the baby crock on low until the barley is tender, about 5 hours.

Squash and Carrot Stew

The squash cooked down and the carrots stayed pretty firm, making an interestingly tasty base to this stew!

Ingredients:
1 cup cubed squash
1/2 cup sliced carrots
1/4 cup diced tomato
1/4 cup seitan
1/2 cup water
1/2 tsp paprika
1/4 tsp cumin
1/4 tsp turmeric
1/4 tsp ginger
1/4 tsp lemon juice
1 mint leaf

Directions:
Place all ingredients in the baby crock on low until the carrots are tender, about 5 hours.

Cauliflower Zucchini Soup

A wonderful taste combination. I shall try a version with white beans soon!

Ingredients:
1/4 cup chopped cauliflower
1/2 cup corn
1/2 cup chopped zucchini
2Tbsp dried black beans
3/4 cup water
Salt
Pepper

Directions:
All ingredients go in the baby crock on low for 4-6 hours.

Vegetarian Cassolet

The rosemary "makes" this dish! Be sure to remove the bay leaf before serving and eating!

Ingredients:
2Tbsp dried beans
1/4 cup chopped carrots
1/4 cup chopped yam
1/2 cup diced mushroom
1/2 cup veggie broth
Bay leaf
3 sprigs parsley
1/2 tsp rosemary
1/4 tsp thyme

Directions:
All ingredients go in the baby crock on low. Cook until beans are tender, about 5 hours.

Coconut Black Bean Stew

The next time I make this, I might crush the coconut for a different texture.

Ingredients:
2Tbsp dried black beans
1/2 cup chopped mushrooms
2Tbsp shredded unsweetened coconut
1/4 tsp paprika
1/4 tsp cumin
1/4 tsp cinnamon
Salt
1/2 cup water

Directions:
Place all ingredients in the baby crock on low until the beans are tender, approximately 4 hours.

Mulligatawny

If you like a little zing, add more ginger and/or more mustard seed. Cardamom is a strong spice, if you add more, it may overpower the combination of flavors. The cinnamon stick gave just a hint of cinnamon, you may want to add ground cinnamon instead.

Ingredients:
1/2 cup chopped carrots
1/2 cup chopped zucchini
1/4 cup chopped yam
1/4 cup chopped cauliflower
1/2 cup diced tomato
2Tbsp dried pinto beans
1/2 cup veggie broth or water
1/4 tsp cardamom
1/4 tsp ginger
1/4 tsp cumin
Salt
Pepper
5 cloves, 1 cinnamon stick, few mustard seeds in a spice ball.

Directions:
Place all ingredients and the spice/tea ball in the baby crock on low for approximately 6 hours. Remove the spice ball before serving.

Veggie Quinoa Chowder

This only took four hours in the crockpot and was tastily filling!

Ingredients:
1/2 cup cubed squash
1/4 cup chopped carrot
1/4 cup peas
1/4 cup cauliflower
1/4 cup diced tomato
1/4 cup chopped zucchini
1/4 cup corn
1Tbsp uncooked quinoa
1/2 cup veggie broth
1/4 tsp ground thyme
1/4 tsp ground ginger
2 sprigs fresh parsley

Directions:
Place all ingredients in the baby crock on low for approximately three hours, or until quinoa is tender.

Three Sisters Stew

This only took my baby crock 5 hours. The cumin makes it very chili-like in taste. I might try it next time without.

Ingredients:
2Tbsp dried pinto beans
1/2 cup corn
1/2 cup diced tomato
1/2 cup water
1/4 tsp cumin
Dash cayenne
Salt
Pepper

Directions:
Place all ingredients in the baby crock on low until the beans are tender.

Indian Bean Risotto

You may want to play with the curry/ginger amounts depending on your tolerance for spicy. My head was pretty clear after this!

Ingredients:
2Tbsp dried white beans
2Tbsp uncooked quinoa
1/2 cup chopped carrot
1/2 cup diced tomato
1/2 tsp cinnamon
1/4 tsp curry powder
1/4 tsp cumin
1/4 tsp ginger
Salt
1 cup water or veggie broth

Directions:
Put all ingredients in the baby crock on low, add more water if needed. Cook until beans are tender.

Potage St. Germaine

A great soup for a chilly evening. I really enjoyed this!

Ingredients:
2Tbsp dried split peas
1/2 cup frozen peas
1/4 cup chopped celery
1/4 cup chopped potato
1/2 cup chopped parsnip
1/2 cup veggie broth
Salt to taste
Ground black pepper to taste

Directions:
Place all ingredients in the baby crock on low until they are very tender. I ate mine this way, but for a smooth, thick soup (the definition of potage), place in a food processor or blender and whir smooth.

Italian Beans

Simple, tasty, filling...what more do you need?

Ingredients:
2Tbsp dried beans
1/2 cup chopped carrot
1/2 cup chopped celery
1/4 tsp oregano
1/2 tsp paprika
Bay leaf
1/2 tsp olive oil
3/4 cup water (add more if needed)
Salt
Pepper

Directions:
Place all ingredients in the baby crock on low until the beans are cooked and tender. Remove the bay leaf before eating.

Crock Pot Sloppy J's

These were an interesting texture, but definitely the flavor of the more recognized "Sloppy Joe." I served mine on baked polenta, but a bun would surely suffice, the recipe makes plenty to make it sloppy!

Ingredients:
1/3 cup dried split peas
1/4 cup diced tomato
1/4 tomato paste
1/2 cup vegetable broth
1 tsp apple cider vinegar
1 tsp parsley
1/2 tsp paprika
1/4 tsp oregano
1/4 tsp cumin
Salt

Directions:
Put all ingredients in the baby crock on low.

Barley Tomato Bean Soup

WOW! The flavors of everything combined beautifully into a filling soup!

Ingredients:
2Tbsp dried white beans
1Tbsp uncooked barley
1/2 cup Lima beans
1/4 cup corn
1/4 cup diced tomato
1/4 cup spinach
1/4 tomato juice/watered sauce
1/2 cup water
Salt
Ground pepper

Directions:

All ingredients go in the baby crock until the beans are tender, about 6 hours.

Vegetable Coconut Curry

This is...so good!! So much better than you would expect it to be! I added and substituted some vegetables in this to make it my very own creation and I am quite proud.

Ingredients:

1 cup squash
1/2 cup peas
1/4 cup parsnips
1/4 cup spinach
1Tbsp coconut shreds
1/4 tsp curry
Salt to taste
1/2 cup water

Directions:

Put all ingredients in the baby crick in low until parsnip is tender, about 4 hours.

Butternut Squash Risotto

You could also use Delicata squash for this. I used the baby crock, but you could do this in a saucepan on the stovetop as well. You may want to substitute cinnamon for the nutmeg. I wasn't overly fond of the flavor of the nutmeg.

Ingredients:

1 cup cubed squash
2Tbsp uncooked quinoa
1/2 tsp vanilla extract
1/4 tsp nutmeg
Salt to taste
1/2 cup water

Directions:

All ingredients go into the baby crock. Cook on low. For me, this only took three hours!

Amalfi Stew

Wow! What a great veggie combo! Carrots and tomatoes!

Ingredients:

2Tbsp dried white beans
1/2 cup tomato sauce
1/4 cup diced tomato
1/2 cup sliced carrots
1/4 cup water
1/2 tsp thyme
Salt to taste

Directions:

Put all ingredients in the baby crock on low until the beans are tender, about 6 hours.

Caponata

I like basil better than oregano, so I used more, but you could change up the amounts of spices however you would like! Serve with toasted or grilled bread.

Ingredients:

1 cup cubed eggplant
1/2 cup sliced celery
1/2 cup canned diced tomato with sauce
2 tsp red wine vinegar
1/4 tsp oregano
1/4 tsp thyme
1/2 tsp rosemary
1/2 tsp basil
1/2 tsp parsley
Salt

Directions:

Sautée eggplant and celery in 1/2 tsp oil for 15 minutes. Add tomato, vinegar, and spices, cover and simmer for 15 minutes.

Tortilla Soup

I added avocado to mine, but I think a dab of sour cream (dairy or non-dairy) would make it even better!

Ingredients:

1/2 cup diced tomatoes with juice (store bought canned or home preserved)
1/2 cup corn
1/4 cup chopped zucchini
2Tbsp dried pinto beans
1/2 cup water
1/4 tsp lime juice
1/4 tsp oregano leaves
1/2 tsp cumin
1/2 tsp paprika
Dash of cayenne pepper
Salt to taste

Tortilla chips, garnishes of choice

Directions:

Place all ingredients (except the chips and garnishes) in the baby crock on low until the beans are just past tender. This took about 7 hours for me. Serve with the garnishes and tortilla chips either on the side or on top!

Black Bean Soup

This is spicy with a hint of clove. Very interesting flavor and a nice soup for a main or a side dish.

Ingredients:

2Tbsp dried black beans
1/2 cup vegetable broth
1/4 cup water
1/2 tsp cumin
1/4 tsp oregano leaves
1/4 tsp thyme
1 clove
salt

Directions:

Place all ingredients in the baby crock on low until the black beans are very tender.

Italian Bean Soup

This is a nicely warming soup for a chilly day. The fennel seed adds an interesting flavor!

Ingredients:

2Tbsp dried white beans (Northern or Navy)
1/4 cup chopped mushrooms
1/4 cup chopped carrots
1/4 cup chopped parsnips
1/4 cup diced tomatos
1/4 cup corn
1/4 cup lima beans
1Tbsp dried split peas
1 cup water
1/4 tsp thyme
1/2 tsp fennel seed
salt
pepper

Directions:

Place all ingredients in the baby crock pot and cook on low until the beans are tender, approximately 6 hours.

Butternut Squash Soup

I'm really impressed with this soup! It's my own creation, made up on the fly. I had some sweet corn still frozen from the summer and I think that put the soup right over the edge into heavenly.

Ingredients:

1/2 cup butternut squash
1/2 cup corn
2Tbsp beans
3/4 cup water or broth
Salt
Pepper

Directions:

Put all ingredients in the baby crock pot and cook on low until the beans are tender. Approximately six hours.

Cincinatti Chili

This is an odd mix and it tastes very interesting! Go ahead and try it, you know you want to!

Ingredients:

2Tbsp dried beans
1/4 seitan
1/2 cup tomato
1/2 cup tomato sauce
1/4 cup water
1/2 tsp cinnamon
1/2 tsp paprika
1/2 tsp cocoa
1/4 tsp cumin
1/4 tsp nutmeg
Pinch ground cloves
Pinch allspice
Pinch cayenne
Salt

Directions:

Crockpot in low until beans are tender.

Mushroom and Pea Risotto

This turned out pretty tasty, though I had a small appliance issue in the cooking! It was supposed to be a crock pot recipe, but after an hour on high in the crock (as recommended), the rice had no indication of cooking at all!

My grocery store happened to have baby Bella mushrooms, which is a very rare occurrence. This recipe could be just button mushrooms with no problem.

Ingredients:

1/4 cup button mushrooms
1/4 cup baby bella mushrooms
1/2 cup peas
2Tbsp rice
1/4 + 1Tbsp water
1/2 tsp oil
Salt
Pepper

Directions:

Put all ingredients in a sauce pan and simmer for about 45 minutes or until the rice is tender. I did have to add a bit more water during the simmer, so keep an eye on it!

Corn Basil "Risotto"

This did not turn out as creamy as a risotto should, but it was still quite tasty. I shall try it again with rice and see if that helps. Though, my next risotto is planned to be a mushroom risotto since I found some baby bellas at the store!

Ingredients:

1 cup kernel corn
2Tbsp quinoa
1/4 cup water or broth
1/2 tsp basil
1/4 tsp thyme
1/4 tsp salt

Directions:

Crockpot on high one hour.

Split Pea Soup

Last night was Sherlock! I wanted to have a quick and easy dinner that I could have eaten and cleaned up so I was ensconced with the dogs and my crocheting on the couch at show time - split pea soup in the baby crock!

I like my split pea soup thick with a bit of "chew," so this recipe can be altered to a more soupy soup by adding more broth or water. Plus, you could whir it in the blender/food processor for a smoother texture.

Ingredients:

1/3 cup dried split peas
1 cup vegetable broth or water (I do make my own veggie broth and you can, too!)
1/4 cut chopped carrots
1 tsp salt
Cracked pepper to garnish

Directions:

Place all ingredients, except the cracked pepper, in the baby crock on low for 6 hours.
Top with cracked pepper to taste at serving.

See? Easy Peasy! Hee Hee!

I did bake a tortilla to serve with it and I had a side of mixed veggies and tofu to complete the meal.

Seitan Ragout

I have been enjoying this season of family, friends, Star Wars, Dr. Who, and the upcoming Sherlock Special! While these activities have been marvelous, one still needs nourishment. This recipe has been altered for one and I have removed the leek and garlic as well. You'll note by the picture that I did get so excited to try it that I forgot to prepare the small salad I was adding for more green! I did not notice until I looked at the very monochromatic picture! This is a baby crock recipe. I do make food that's crock pot, it's just that the activities of this week and the weather have been so conducive to this fun little kitchen appliance.

Ingredients:

1/2 cup sliced carrots
1/4 cup diced rutabaga (could substitute turnips or eliminate and use more potato)
1/4 diced potato
1/2 cup veggie broth
1/2 tsp marjoram
Salt
Pepper

Directions:

Put all ingredients in the crock pot and give it a good stir. Cook on low until the veggies are tender. It took mine about 5 hours. I did add some arrowroot to thicken up the remaining broth for a thicker ragout!

I served with quinoa and mixed beans as well as a nice green salad (not pictured).

Squash Minestrone

As you can see, I'm following my "Squash is Delightful" theme throughout the week! Actually, I bought a butternut squash and it has plenty of single servings in it. In the past, I've baked it and then frozen portions. This time, I wanted it raw so I could crockpot with it. I've chosen to cook it in a variety of ways, however, so it is not getting "old" at all!

This minestrone recipe can be used all year long with whatever vegetables are seasonally available. The spices make it POP! I will say, this meal made me very, very full! Come hungry to the table.

Ingredients:

1/3 cup squash cubed
1/3 cup celery chopped
1/3 cup carrots chopped
1 cup tomato sauce
2Tbsp white beans
1/2 water
1/4 tsp oregano leaves
1/4 tsp marjoram leave
1/4 tsp rosemary leaves
1 tsp salt

*** A note *** If you're tomato sauce is more watery, add less water. Mine is homemade and was pureed. It needed a bit of water for those beans to absorb.

Directions:

Add all ingredients to the baby crock and cook on low for 4-6 hours, until your beans are the desired tenderness.

I served mine with toasted polenta and pan fried firm tofu.

Butternut Squash Soup

I have discovered squash. Yes, I know I'm coming to it late. I blame acorn squash. I really, really dislike acorn squash and that intense dislike has kept me from trying other types...until this Autumn. Now I'm having an affair with squashes not acorn! Keeping in the theme of warming the inside using the baby crock, I made butternut squash soup and it was num yummers. I like my soups with a bit of chew potential so I just let this cook down naturally. If you like it smoother, you can whir it up in the blender or food processor.

Ingredients:
1 cup squash
1/2 cup water
1/2 tsp cinnamon
1/2 tsp salt
1/8 tsp nutmeg

Directions:
Add all ingredients to the crock pot and give it a stir. Cook on low for 4-6 hours until the squash is cooked to your preference. It will need to be quite soft to whir up smooth.

I served this with homemade baked tortilla chips, sauteed zucchini with mushrooms, and a mixture of pinto beans, great northern beans, and black beans.

Chili

The weather has gotten a bit colder around these parts so I'm using my baby crock for "warming the inside" meals. I have so tell you, I adore the baby crock! Perfect for cooking meals for one or two.

This recipe is for the chili I made the other night. It turned out perfectly for me! I had to pat myself on the back after I ate it from pride! I'm sure you'll be just as pleased.

Ingredients:
2 tbsp pinto beans
1/4 cup spiced Seitan
1 cup tomato sauce with diced tomatoes
1tsp cumin
1/2 tsp paprika
Cayenne to taste
Salt to taste

Avocado
Cheese or choice

Directions:
Add all ingredients except cheese and avocado to the crock pot. If you would like this to be more soup-like, add 1/4 - 1/2 cup water. I like mine nice and thick, so I let my beans soak up the juice from the tomato sauce. This took only 5 hours to be ready!

Pour into a bowl and garnish with avocado and your cheese of choice. I used mozzarella!

I served this with homemade baked tortilla chips and a small mixed salad.

Curried Apple Seitan!

Ingredients:
1/4 Seitan - mixed with curry and cinnamon, but left not boiled.
1 spoonful of Apple sauce or 2Tbsp chunked fresh apple
1 1/2 cups diced carrot
1/2 cup vegetable broth
Two dashes of Curry
1/2 tsp Cinnamon
1/4 tsp Ginger
Salt to taste
1Tbsp Coconut

Directions:
Place all ingredients into the baby crock pot, reserving about 1/2 the Tbsp coconut for garnish.
Cook on low for approximately 6 hours or until your carrots are tender. The broth should be
mostly cooked away, but I served mine in a bowl to catch whatever remained. You could serve
over quinoa to solve any juice issues as well! I plated mine with tofu and quinoa.

Veggie Stew

A great dish for chasing the winter chill away. Full of hearty root vegetables tossed in the baby crock, your living space will fill up with the good smells while you anticipate dinner!

Ingredients:
1/2 cup carrot, sliced thin
1/2 cup parsnip
1/2 cup turnip
1/2 cup rutabaga
2 tbsp navy beans
1/4 seitan
1/2 tsp. cinnamon
1/4 tsp. nutmeg and sage
A twist or two of black peppercorn
Salt to taste.

All ingredients go in the baby crock for approximately 6 hours, or until the veggies are the tenderness you prefer.

Note:
I added about 1/4 tsp. arrowroot to thicken up the gravy a bit.

Served with a slice of sourdough!

In the Oven

Roasted Rosemary Sweet Potato and Parsnip

This is a great combination. You will need to have a protein side dish!

Ingredients:
1/2 cup cubed sweet potato
1/2 cup parsnip
1/2 tsp rosemary
oil
salt to tasted

Directions:
 Mix the parsnip and sweet potato and toss with oil and rosemary. Place on a baking sheet and bake at 350 degrees for 30 minutes or until the ingredients are soft.

Spinach, Tomato, Corn Taco

You could also put this in the oven and bake it for about 20 minutes.

Ingredients:
1/2 cup cooked spinach
1/2 cup diced tomato
1/4 cup corn
1/4 tsp cumin
1/4 tsp paprika
Salt
Tortilla

Directions:
Set aside the tortilla. Sautee the remaining ingredients together until the tomato is soft. Spoon into the tortilla and serve.

Califredo Pizza

Pasta pizza! This was a radical idea I thought I would try with the crust instead of the noodles. YUM!

Ingredients:
Crust dough
1/2 cup cooked white beans
1/2 cup cooked cauliflower
1/4 cup sliced tomato
1/4 cup water
1/2 tsp oil
Cracked pepper
Salt

Directions:
Put the white beans, cauliflower, water, oil, pepper, and salt into a food processor or blender and whir it smooth. Press or roll the crust dough into a shape close to a circle on a piece of parchment paper on a baking sheet. Spread the caulifredo sauce on the crust and top with the tomatoes. Bake at 400 degrees for 20 minutes or until the crust is golden brown. It may take a bit longer due to the moisture in the sauce.

Gritty Eggplant

Interesting casserole. I enjoyed it!

Ingredients:
1/2 cup prepared grits
1 cup peeled and diced eggplant
1/2 cup diced tomato

Directions:
Sautee the eggplant and tomato with a bit of oil until the tomato is soft. Mix in with the grits and pour into a small greased baking dish. Bake at 400 degrees for 20 minutes.

Breakfast Pizza

Ingredients
Crust dough
1/4 cup diced tomato
1/4 cup diced mushroom
1 Egg

Directions
Roll or press out the dough into a round on a parchment paper piece on a baking sheet. Bake at 400 degrees for 20 minutes or until golden brown. Scramble the egg, tomato, and mushroom and add salt to taste. Spoon the egg mixture on the crust and serve!

Sauerkraut Kugel

A taste of Germany in a crusty pocket!

Ingredients:
Crust dough
1/2 cup sauerkraut
1/4 cup diced and cooked potato
1/4 cup corn

Directions:
Press the dough out on a piece of parchment paper on a baking sheet. Press it as circular as you can, or roll it out, 1/4" thickness. Mix the rest of the ingredients and spoon into the center. Pull the edges of the dough up and pinch them so only a small circle of the ingredients is visible. Bake at 400 degrees for 20 minutes or until the crust is golden brown.

Baked Cauliflower with Mushroom Gravy

Very good and surprisingly easy to prepare!

Ingredients:
1 cup cauliflower florets (I used frozen)
1/4 cup diced mushrooms
1/4 tsp thyme
1/4 tsp oregano
salt
pepper
 arrowroot

Directions:
Toss the cauliflower with a bit of oil, the thyme, the oregano, salt, and pepper. Bake on a sheet at 400 degrees for 30 minutes. While the cauliflower is baking, put the mushrooms in about 1/2 cup of water and boil for 10 minutes. Add arrowroot (or cornstarch) to thicken to a gravy. Salt this to your taste preference. Put the cauliflower on a plate when it's baked and pour the gravy over it.

Cabbage Pie with Mashed Potato

This pie is good this way, too!

Ingredients:
1 cup shredded cabbage
1/4 cup corn
1/4 cup potato
1 ounce firm tofu

Directions:
Boil the cabbage and corn for 20 minutes, drain. Boil and mash the potatoes. Put the cabbage and corn in a small, greased baking dish. Mix the mashed potatoes and tofu and spread on top. Bake at 400 degrees for 20 minutes.

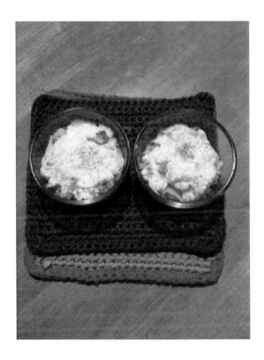

Grits and Egg Casserole

Grits baked in the oven are one of my new favorite things.

Ingredients:
1/2 cup prepared grits
1 egg
1/4 cup diced seitan
1/4 cup corn
1/4 cup diced tomato
Salt to taste

Directions:
Mix the ingredients thoroughly and pour into a greased baking dish. Bake at 400 degrees for 20 minutes.

Mexican Street Tortillas

Tasty handheld goodness! I added some cheese to mine.

Ingredients
1/2 cup corn
1/2 cup cooked refried beans
corn tortilla
Cumin to taste

Directions:
Cut the tortilla into quarters and place on a baking sheet. Top with the refried beans, then the corn, and then sprinkle cumin on top. Bake at 350 for 20 minutes or until the tortilla is crispy.

Cabbage Rolls

A tasty dish, somewhat difficult to eat!

Ingredients:
2 cabbage leaves
1/4 cup cooked quinoa
1/4 cup cooked pinto beans
1/2 cup tomato sauce
1/2 tsp red wine vinegar
Salt to taste

Directions:
Steam the cabbage rolls until tender. Mix the quinoa, pinto beans, red wine vinegar, and salt. Spoon the mixture into the cabbage rolls and roll them gently. Spoon 1/4 cup of the tomato sauce into a baking dish. Place the cabbage rolls in the dish, seam side down. Spoon the rest of the sauce over the top of the rolls. Bake at 350 degrees for 30 minutes.

Mexican Pizza

There's something about the corn that just adds so much to this pizza!

Ingredients:
Crust dough
1/2 cup cooked and pureed black beans
1/4 tsp cumin
1/4 tsp paprika
1/4 cup corn
1/4 cup diced tomato
1/4 cup shredded lettuce
Salt to taste

Directions:
Mix the cumin and paprika in the black bean puree. Roll or press out the crust dough in a circular shape. Spread the black bean paste on the crust. Top with the corn and tomato. Bake at 400 degrees for 20 minutes. Before serving, top with the shredded lettuce.

Cauliflower with Potato

This is actually a Russian dish, though you cannot tell from the name.

Ingredients:
1/2 cup cooked cauliflower in small pieces
1/2 cup cooked potato, diced
1 egg
1 Tbsp flour

Directions:
Mix all ingredients thoroughly. Add salt and pepper to taste. Spoon into a small, greased baking dish. Bake at 400 degrees for 20 minutes.

Burrito

Ingredients:
1/4 cup black bean puree
1/4 seitan
1/4 tsp cumin
1/4 tsp paprika

Directions:
Sautee the seitan with the spices. Mix with the black bean puree. Spread on a tortilla and roll.
Place seam side down in a baking dish and bake at 350 for 30 minutes.

Cabbage Pie

Be sure you stew the cabbage first, it may use up the water, just add a touch more.

Ingredients:
Crust dough
1 cup cabbage, shredded
1/4 cup sliced carrot (substitute corn for a different taste)
1 ounce firm tofu, cubed
salt to taste

Directions:
Stew the cabbage and carrots with 1/2 cup water for 20 minutes. Drain. Add salt and pepper. Put into a baking dish or small glass bowls. Top with the dough. Bake at 400 degrees for 20 minutes or until the crust is golden brown.

Roasted Cabbage

This dish can be a main dish, but you'll need to add a protein and a grain as sides. When I make this again, I may top it with tofu. I used two slices when I prepared it because my first slice was an end and I cut it pretty thin!

Ingredients:
1 1" slice of cabbage
1/2 tsp caraway seeds
Bit of oil

Directions:
Put the cabbage in a baking dish, toss the caraway seeds on the cabbage slice, and drizzle with oil. Bake at 400 degrees for 40 minutes.

Butternut Grits Casserole

You can't go wrong with grits!

Ingredients:
1/2 cup cubed cooked butternut squash
1/2 cup diced tomato
1/2 cup corn
1/2 cup black beans
1 package prepared grits

Directions:
Mix the ingredients in a small bowl with salt, pepper, and a dash of cayenne pepper. Spoon the mixture into a greased baking dish and bake at 350 degrees for 20 minutes.

Reuben Pizza

My own creation. I don't really like Thousand Island dressing, so I created my own Reuben dressing which also adds a protein. However, you could substitute Thousand Island.

Ingredients:
Crust dough
1/2 cup sauerkraut
1/4 cup diced seitan
1/4 tsp caraway seeds
1 ounce firm tofu
1 tsp tomato sauce
1/4 tsp mustard powder
salt
pepper
dash cayenne pepper

Directions:
Roll or press the crust dough out into a circular shape and sprinkle with the caraway seeds. Sautee the seitan with salt and pepper and a bit of oil until it's just crunchy and set aside. Put the tofu, tomato sauce, mustard powder, salt, pepper, and cayenne in a small bowl and mix with enough water to make a thick sauce. Put the sauerkraut in a layer on the crust, add the seitan, then top with the sauce. Bake at 400 degrees for 20 minutes or until the crust is golden brown.

Baked Parsnips

The next time I make this, I will leave off the nutmeg (I'm not a big fan).

Ingredients:
1 cup sliced parsnips
1 ounce firm tofu, cubed
1/4 cup black beans
salt to taste
pinch of nutmeg

Directions:
Boil the parsnips until they are tender. Combine with 1 Tbsp veggie broth or water in a baking dish. Sprinkle with salt, perhaps a bit of pepper, and the pinch of nutmeg. Bake at 350 degrees for 30 minutes.

Mushroom Noodle Bake

Another Russian dish. It is really easy to make and very tasty!

Ingredients:
1/2 cup sliced mushrooms
1 ounce firm tofu, cubed
1/4 cup noodles of choice (I used fettucini)
1 egg
Cheese of choice (about 1Tbsp)
1Tbsp cornmeal

Directions:
 Mix all ingredients except for the cornmeal. Pour into a small greased baking dish, or I used two small glass bowls. Sprinkle the cornmeal on top and bake at 400 degrees for 20 minutes.

Eggplant Pinto Bean Casserole

This is actually a Russian recipe!

Ingredients:
1 cup peeled and cubed eggplant
1/2 cup diced tomato
1/2 cup cooked pinto beans
1/4 cup tomato sauce
1/4 tsp thyme
Salt to taste

Directions:
Mix the ingredients and spoon into a greased baking dish. Bake at 350 degrees for 20 minutes.

Colcannon

The baking dish I used (you can see it in the picture) is a bit too large for this, I would choose something smaller.

Ingredients:
1/2 cup diced potato
1 cup kale
1 ounce firm tofu
salt
pepper

Directions:
Boil the potato until tender. Chop the kale small and steam until tender in the microwave, about 1 minute. Mix the tofu with a bit of water until you have a smooth sauce. Mash the potatoes and mix in the kale, salt, pepper, and tofu sauce. Spoon into a greased baking dish and bake at 350 degrees for 15 minutes.

Mexican Cornbread Pie

My own creation...turned out very well.

Ingredients:
Cornbread:
3Tbsp cornmeal
1Tbsp flour
1/2 tsp baking powder
pinch baking soda
pinch salt
1/2 tsp oil
1Tbsp milk
1Tbsp + 1tsp water

The rest:
1/2 cup corn
1/2 cup diced tomato
1/2 cup butternut squash (or pumpkin)
1/2 cup black beans
1/4 tsp cumin
1/4 tsp paprika
salt to taste

Directions:
Mix the cornbread in a separate bowl and set aside. Mix the rest of the ingredients and put them into a small greased baking dish. Spoon the cornbread mixture over the top and bake at 400 degrees for 20 minutes.

Caulifredo Pizza

Pasta pizza! This was a radical idea I thought I would try with the crust instead of the noodles. YUM!

Ingredients:
Crust dough
1/2 cup cooked white beans
1/2 cup cooked cauliflower
1/4 cup sliced tomato
1/4 cup water
1/2 tsp oil
Cracked pepper
Salt

Directions:
Put the white beans, cauliflower, water, oil, pepper, and salt into a food processor or blender and whir it smooth. Press or roll the crust dough into a shape close to a circle on a piece of parchment paper on a baking sheet. Spread the caulifredo sauce on the crust and top with the tomatoes. Bake at 400 degrees for 20 minutes or until the crust is golden brown. It may take a bit longer due to the moisture in the sauce.

Gritty Eggplant

Interesting casserole. I enjoyed it!

Ingredients:
1/2 cup prepared grits
1 cup peeled and diced eggplant
1/2 cup diced tomato

Directions:
Sautee the eggplant and tomato with a bit of oil until the tomato is soft. Mix in with the grits and pour into a small greased baking dish. Bake at 400 degrees for 20 minutes.

Breakfast Pizza

Ingredients
Crust dough
1/4 cup diced tomato
1/4 cup diced mushroom
1 Egg

Directions
Roll or press out the dough into a round on a parchment paper piece on a baking sheet. Bake at 400 degrees for 20 minutes or until golden brown. Scramble the egg, tomato, and mushroom and add salt to taste. Spoon the egg mixture on the crust and serve!

Sauerkraut Kugel

A taste of Germany in a crusty pocket!

Ingredients:
Crust dough
1/2 cup sauerkraut
1/4 cup diced and cooked potato
1/4 cup corn

Directions:
Press the dough out on a piece of parchment paper on a baking sheet. Press it as circular as you can, or roll it out, 1/4" thickness. Mix the rest of the ingredients and spoon into the center. Pull the edges of the dough up and pinch them so only a small circle of the ingredients is visible. Bake at 400 degrees for 20 minutes or until the crust is golden brown.

Italian 3 Squash Bake

This had an interesting flavor, but in the future, I might add more of the spices.

Ingredients:
1/2 cup cubed cooked acorn squash
1/2 cup cubed cooked pumpkin
1/2 cup cubed cooked butternut squash
1/2 cup diced tomato
1/4 tsp sage
1/4 tsp thyme
Sprinkle of cinnamon for the top
Salt to taste
Cheese of choice

Directions:
Mix the squashes, tomato, and spices and put in a greased baking dish. Sprinkle the cinnamon.
Top with the cheese. Bake at 350 for 20 minutes.

Grits and Greens

This is fantastic! You could substitute cooked spinach if you cannot find kale.

Ingredients:
1 cup kale
1/2 cup prepared grits
1 egg
cheese of choice
1/4 cup Rotel
Salt to taste

Directions:
Cook the kale in a bit of water just until wilted. Strain it out and put to the side. Mix the grits, egg, cheese, and Rotel. Spoon half the mixture into a greased baking dish. Put the kale in a layer on top. Cover with the remaining grits mixture. Bake at 400 for 20 minutes. Let stand for 10 additional minutes before serving.

Butternut Squash Casserole

If you cut your butternut squash early, you can roast the seeds and use those in place of the pumpkin seeds.

Ingredients:
1 cup uncooked butternut squash, cubed
1/2 cup cooked spinach
1/4 cup cooked quinoa
1 ounce firm tofu cubed
2Tbsp pumpkin seeds
1/4 tsp sage
Salt to taste
1/4 cup water

Directions:
Boil the squash until tender. Transfer the squash to a skillet and add the sage, salt, and water. Simmer until the squash is breaking down and creamy (you may have to add more water). Add the quinoa, spinach, and tofu. Mix well. Transfer the mixture to a greased baking dish and top with the pumpkin seeds. Cover and bake at 400 degrees for 10 minutes. Remove the cover and cook for another 5 minutes.

Grits Casserole

Don't forget to grease your baking dish, grits get sticky, bless their hearts.

Ingredients:
1/2 cup prepared grits
1/2 cup corn
1/2 cup diced tomato
1/2 cup black beans
Cheese (optional)

Directions:
Combine the ingredients, except the cheese. Salt to taste. Spoon the mixture into a greased baking dish and top with the cheese. Bake at 400 degrees for 20 minutes.

Carrot Squash Casserole

Something about dill and carrots together is just...right. Excellent way to use winter veggies.

Ingredients:
1 cup sliced carrots
1/2 cup cubed butternut squash
1 Tbsp cornmeal
2 Tbsp Nutritional Yeast
1 ounce firm tofu
1/4 tsp dill
Salt
Water

Directions:
In a saucepan, simmer the carrots and squash until they are tender. While they are cooking, make a thick sauce with the Nutritional Yeast, tofu, dill, and salt to taste. Put the tender carrots and squash in a greased baking dish and top with the tofu dill sauce. Sprinkle with the cornmeal. Bake at 350 for 25 minutes.

Pumpkin Spinach Lasagna

In this recipe, you could replace the Nutritional Yeast Tofu sauce with the shredded cheese of you choice.

Ingredients:
1/2 cup cubed pumpkin
1/2 cup pureed pumpkin
1/2 cup cooked spinach
2 Tbsp Nutritional Yeast
1 ounce firm tofu

Directions:
Mix the nutritional yeast and tofu with enough water to make a thick sauce. Add salt to taste. In a greased baking dish, layer half the spinach, then the half the puree, then half the cubes, and half the sauce...repeat. Bake at 350 for 30 minutes.

Cauliflower Tacos

This was amazing! Taste and texture perfect for a taco!

Ingredients:
1/2 cup cooked cauliflower
1/2 cup mushroom
1/4 tsp cumin
1/4 tsp paprika
Salt
Water
Taco shell

Directions:
Put the cauliflower in the food processor and whir until it resembles rice. Scrape it into a bowl.
Put the mushrooms in the food processor and lightly whir until crumbly. Combine with the
cauliflower and mix in the spices. Add just enough water to make the mixture clump together.
Spoon on to a parchment paper lined baking sheet and bake at 350 for 15 minutes, remove and
stir, and continue to bake for another 15 minutes. Spoon the baked mixture into your taco shell,
garnish as desired, and eat!

Stuffed Acorn Squash #2

One could add some cumin to the mix and give these a Mexican flavor. They are delicious just the way they are presented, though!

Ingredients:
1 small acorn squash
1/2 cup cooked black beans
1/2 cup corn
1/2 cup diced tomato
1/4 cup cooked quinoa

Directions:
Halve and de-seed the acorn squash. Bake it face up at 400 degrees for 30-45 minutes. Mix the remaining ingredients and heat through using the microwave, about 1 minute. Remove the acorn squash from the oven and spoon the filling mixture in each half. Serve!

Corn Mush Pie

My own creation, a version of shepherd's pie.

Ingredients:
2Tbsp cornmeal
1/2 cup water

1/4 cup corn
1/2 cup cooked black beans
1/4 cup diced potato
1/4 cup peas
1/4 cup diced carrot

Directions:
Mix the cornmeal in the water and microwave it until the liquid is absorbed (in 30 second intervals, stirring between each, it takes about 2 minutes) and a mush has formed. Mix the rest of the ingredients into the mush and put into a small baking dish that has been greased. Bake at 350 degrees for 25 minutes.

Acorn Squash Pizza

The spices on this provide an interesting twist!

Ingredients:
Crust dough
1/2 cup acorn squash cooked and pureed
1/4 cup sliced tomato
1/4 cup sliced mushroom
1/4 tsp sage
1/4 tsp rosemary

Directions:
Roll or press out dough on a greased or lined baking sheet. Spread the crust with the acorn squash and top with the sage and rosemary. Layer on the tomato and mushrooms. Bake at 400 degrees for 20 minutes or until the crust is golden brown.

Tin Foil Dinner

When I was smallish and we camped, these were called "hobo packets!"

Ingredients:
 1/2 cup cubed acorn squash
1/4 cup diced potato
1/4 cup corn
1/4 cup sliced carrot
1/4 cup green beans
1/4 cup zucchini or yellow squash
1/4 cup diced mushroom
1/4 cup seitan, chopped (optional)
1/2 tsp oil
Salt
Pepper

Directions:
Cut off a medium sized piece of tin foil. Use a non-stick spray to "grease" it. Place all the ingredients on the center of the foil. Top with the oil and salt and pepper to taste. Fold the tin foil around the vegetables so everything is covered and the edges are crimped. I put mine on a baking sheet in case of leaks. Bake in the oven at 400 degrees for 40 minutes.

Broiled Tomato and Eggplant Sandwich

I put my bread in with the eggplant and tomato to make my toast.

Ingredients:
2 slices tomato
2 slices eggplant
1 ounce firm tofu, sliced
2 leaves basil
bread of choice

Directions:
Put the eggplant and tomato slices on a broiler pan and broil for five minutes on each side. Place the slices on the toast and top with the tofu and basil. Broil for an additional two minutes. I cut my bread in half for easier handling.

Spinach Mushroom Pizza

What a great combination!

Ingredients:
Crust dough
1/2 cup chopped cooked spinach
1/4 cup sliced mushroom
1 ounce sliced firm tofu

Directions:
Roll or press crust dough out on a greased or lined baking sheet. Top with the spinach, layer on the mushrooms, then the last layer is the tofu. Salt and pepper to taste. Bake at 400 degrees for 20 minutes or until the crust is golden brown.

Stuffed Acorn Squash

Seriously delicious. I salted my acorn squash before cooking.

Ingredients:
1 small to medium acorn squash
1/2 cup cooked cauliflower
1/2 cup kale
Salt
Pepper

Directions:
Cut the squash in half and scoop the seeds out. Place the halved face up on a baking sheet and bake at 400 degrees for 30-45 minutes.
While the squash is baking, put the cauliflower in a food processor and whir to rice-like consistency. Sautée the cauliflower with the kale in a bit of oil, salt and pepper to taste, until the kale is limp. When the squash is baked, spoon this mixture into each half and serve!

Zucchini Enchiladas

I like to sautee the zucchini first as it absorbs the flavor from the other vegetables and becomes the ultimate in yum.

Ingredients:
1/2 cup diced zucchini
1/4 cup diced mushroom
1/4 cup diced red bell pepper
Tortilla

Directions:
Sautée the veggies with a bit of oil and salt until the zucchini is tender. Spoon the mixture into the tortilla. Roll and place seam side down in a baking dish. Bake at 350 for 15 minutes.

Eggplant Pizza

I sautee the veggies first in order to fully incorporate the spices and let the eggplant soak them up!

Ingredients:
Crust dough

1/2 cup peeled and cubed eggplant
1/2 cup diced tomato
1 ounce diced firm tofu
1/8 tsp oregano
1/8 tsp basil
1/8 tsp thyme

Directions:
Sautée all but the crust dough together until the eggplant is tender. Roll or press out the dough in a circle on parchment paper placed on a baking sheet. Top with the sautéed veggies. Bake at 400 degrees for 20 minutes or until the crust is golden brown.

Thai Curry Pizza

I added the spices to the sauce to make sure they carried the pizza and didn't overwhelm it, but you may wish to sprinkle some on top.

Ingredients:
Crust dough
1 ounce firm tofu, sliced
1/4 tomato sauce
1/4 cup sliced tomato
1/2 cup sliced carrots
1/2 cup sliced zucchini
1/4 tsp curry
1/8 tsp ginger
Salt

Directions:
Roll or press out the dough in a circle. Mix the curry and ginger into the tomato sauce and spread on the dough. Add the tomatoes, then the zucchini, the carrots, and top with tofu. Salt to taste and sprinkle with a pinch of curry. Bake at 400 degrees for 20 minutes or until the crust is golden brown.

Eggplant Bake

Eggplant goes so very well with tomato!

Ingredients:
1 cup cubed and peeled eggplant
1/2 cup diced tomato
1 ounce firm tofu, cubed
1/4 tsp thyme
3 leaves basil, chopped
 Salt

Directions:
Mix all thoroughly. Spoon into a greased baking dish. Bake at 350 degrees for 20 minutes.

Vegetable Tian

This will take the full 30 minutes, perhaps a bit longer, for the potatoes to become tender.

Ingredients:
1/4 cup sliced potato
1/4 cup sliced sweet potato
1/2 cup sliced zucchini
1/2 cup sliced tomato
1/4 tsp thyme
Salt
Pepper

Directions:
Layer the veggies in a greased baking dish. Sprinkle the top with the thyme. Salt and pepper to taste. Bake at 375 degrees for 30 minutes or until the potatoes are tender.

Corn Zucchini Tomato Galette

These are just such fun little pockets!

Ingredients:
Crust dough
1/2 cup cooked corn
1/2 cup diced zucchini
1/2 cup diced tomato
Salt to taste

Directions:
Roll or press out the dough in a circle.
Mix the veggies. Spoon the mixture into the center of the dough. Fold up the edges so only a small portion of the mixture is visible. Bake at 400 degrees for 20 minutes or until the crust is golden brown.

Eggplant Casserole

This is amazing!

Ingredients:
1 cup cubed and peeled eggplant
1/4 cup seitan
1/4 cup diced tomato
1/4 cup diced mushroom
2 Tbsp milk
1 egg
2 Tbsp cornmeal
1/2 tsp oil
Salt to taste

Directions:
Boil the eggplant until tender and let cool. Sautée the seitan until crisp. Mix all but the cornmeal thoroughly. Pour into a greased baking dish. Top with the cornmeal. Bake at 375 degrees for 30 minutes.

Zucchini Eggplant Bake

The eggplant "made" this dish. In the future, I may use more basil.

Ingredients:
1 cup cubed and peeled eggplant
1/2 cup sliced tomato
1/2 cup sliced zucchini
1 ounce firm tofu
1/4 tsp oregano
3 leaves of basil
Salt to taste
Cheese of choice

Directions:
Sautée the eggplant with s bit of oil and oregano. Put in a baking dish and top with the cheese. Top this with alternating layers of tomato and zucchini. Last layer is the sliced tofu. Three leaves of basil to finish up. Bake at 425 for 25 minutes.

Zucchini Strata

You could also microwave this. I used two glass bowls and I cooked one in the oven for 20 minutes. The other cooked in the microwave in about 4 minutes. However, the oven baked one had a nice crusty texture on top that the microwaved one did not.

Ingredients:
1 cup diced or cubed zucchini
1 slice polenta
1 egg

Directions:
Combine the zucchini and egg and mix well. Salt to taste. Pour In a small baking dish (I use two glass bowls) and drop in the polenta. Bake at 375 for 20 minutes or until golden brown on top.

Black Bean Butternut Squash Flauta

 The filling can be used in more than one tortilla, or you can do what I did and spread it around the one tortilla in the baking dish.

Ingredients:
1/2 cup cooked black beans
1/2 cup cooked butternut squash (or sweet potato or pumpkin)
1/4 cup corn
1/4 cup tomato
Salt to taste
Tortilla

Directions:
Mix the ingredients. Spray a non-stick spray (or lightly brush with melted butter) one side of the tortilla. Flip it over and fill it with the mix. Roll it up and place it seam side down in a baking dish. Bake at 425 degrees for 15 minutes.

Tomato Zucchini Galette

Fresh zucchini and fresh tomato....so good!

Ingredients:
Crust dough
1/2 cup diced tomato
1/2 cup diced zucchini
Salt to taste

Directions:
Roll or press the dough out into a circle. Mix the zucchini and tomato and put them in the center of the dough. Press the edges up around the mix. Make sure your creation is on a lightly greased baking sheet or on a parchment paper lined baking sheet. Bake at 400 degrees for 20 minutes or until the crust is lightly browned.

Taco Boat

A handy vegetable shell, to be sure!

Ingredients:
1/2 medium zucchini sliced lengthwise
1/4 cup taco seitan
1/4 cup diced tomato
1 ounce firm tofu, cubed
Cheese
1/4 tsp cumin
1/4 tsp paprika
Salt

Directions:
Scoop the seedy middle out of the zucchini. Mix the seitan, tomato, and spices. Fill the zucchini boat and top with your cheese of choice. Bake at 425 degrees for 15 minutes. Top with 1/4 shredded lettuce and serve!

Sweet Corn Pizza

Fresh sweet corn is abundant this time of year and I suggest it and fresh tomatoes for this pizza. However, I imagine any corn would be good!

Ingredients:
Crust dough
1 cup corn
3 leaves fresh basil
1 ounce firm tofu, cubed
1/4 cup diced tomato

Directions:
Roll or press the dough into a circle. Mix the basil, corn, tomato, and tofu. Spread the mixture over the crust. Bake at 400 degrees for 15 minutes or until crust is golden brown.

Zucchini Egg Boat

These zucchini boats are my new favorite thing!

Ingredients:
1/2 medium zucchini sliced lengthwise
1 egg
1 ounce firm tofu cubed
1/2 cup diced tomato
1/2 cup diced mushroom

Directions:
Scoop out the middle of the zucchini, leaving a good portion of flesh. Mix the zucchini insides, egg, tofu, tomato, and mushroom. Pour the mixture in the boat. Bake at 425 for 15 minutes or until the egg is cooked through.

Zucchini Pizza

I had an evening where it cooled down rapidly and I had all this zucchini...so I used the oven to create pizza!

Ingredients:
1/2 cup butternut squash purée
1/2 cup sliced zucchini
1/4 cup sliced mushroom
1 ounce sliced firm tofu
Dash oregano
Salt
Pepper

Crust dough

Directions:
Roll dough out into a circle on parchment paper on a baking sheet. Spread the purée on the crust. Add the oregano. Top with zucchini, mushrooms, and tofu. Salt and pepper to taste. Bake at 400 degrees for 20 minutes or until the crust is golden brown.

Pizza Boat

Zucchini is growing like mad in the garden. I was given a recipe for zucchini boats and I have done my thing and altered it! You will have "stuffing" left over. I just ate mine on the side!

Ingredients:
1/2 a medium zucchini cut lengthwise
1/4 cup chopped seitan
1/2 cup tomato sauce
1/4 cup chopped mushroom
1/4 cup chopped spinach
1 ounce firm tofu, cubed
Salt
Pepper
1/4 tsp parsley
Dash oregano
Dash thyme

Directions:
Scrape out the seeds from the zucchini, leaving the flesh. Chop this up and put it in your pizza mix. Sautée the seitan in a bit of oil, salt, parsley, and pepper until crisp.
Mix the sauce, seitan, tofu, mushrooms, and spinach with the oregano and thyme in a bowl. Spoon it into the boat. Put the boat on a baking sheet and bake at 425 for 10 to 15 minutes.

Radish Pizza

This is an original recipe and I have to say it turned out quite well. The black beans can be easily pureed with a fork. I would save this for a night that isn't going to be really warm as it uses the oven!

Ingredients:
Crust dough
1/2 cup cooked black beans puréed
1/2 cup sliced radish
4 leaves fresh basil
Salt

Directions:
Roll out the crust dough on a baking sheet in a circle. Spread the black bean purée on the crust. Lay the radishes out on top of the purée. Top with the basil leaves. Bake in the oven at 400 degrees for 20 minutes or until the crust is golden brown.

Chimichanga

This was tasty! You could add whatever sides you like to this, like avocado and/or cheese.

Ingredients:
1/4 cup cooked refried beans
1/4 cup cooked black beans
1/2 cup diced mushrooms
1/2 cup diced tomato
1/4 teaspoon cumin
Salt

Directions:
Sautée mushrooms with cumin. Add the remaining ingredients and cook until heated. Spoon in tortilla. Roll tortilla. Placed the tortilla seam side down on a baking sheet and cook at 400° for 15 minutes.

Spaghetti Squash Pizza

A gluten free, lactose free meal that has all the flavor you could possibly want! Amazingly delicious.

Ingredients:
1 cup cooked spaghetti squash
1 oz firm tofu
1 egg
1/2 cup butternut squash purée
1/4 cup sliced tomato
1/4 cup sliced mushroom
Salt
Pepper

Directions:
Mix the spaghetti squash, tofu, and egg. Line a baking sheet with parchment paper. Pour the mix on to the parchment paper and shape in a circle. Bake at 425 degrees for 20 minutes. Remove from oven.
Spread the squash purée on the crust. Top with tomato and mushroom. Bake for ten more minutes.

Zucchini Summer Squash Spinach Bake

Very tasty, quick prep, but it will heat up the kitchen!

Ingredients:
1/2 cup sliced zucchini
1/2 cup sliced summer squash
1/2 cup cooked spinach
1/2 cup sliced tomato
2Tbsp Nutritional Yeast
1 oz tofu

Directions
Make a sauce with the yeast, tofu, and a bit of water. Layer zucchini, squash, spinach, and tomato in a small baking dish. Top with sauce. Bake at 350 degrees for 30 minutes.

Pot Pie

The preparation is a bit lengthy, but the result is amazing!

Ingredients:
Crust dough (earlier entry)

1/2 cup green beans
1/4 cup cubed sweet potato
1/4 cup chopped mushroom
1/4 cup corn
1/4 cup peas
1/4 cup chopped carrot
1/4 cup chopped radish
3/4 cup veggie broth
1/4 cup white bean.

Directions:
Simmer all ingredients except beans until tender. Thicken the broth with a bit of arrowroot or flour. Add the beans. Spoon into a small baking dish (I use two glass bowls). Roll the crust into a square and poke ventilation holes in it. Lay it on top of the mixture in the baking dish. Bake at 400 degrees for 20 minutes or until the crust is golden brown.

Squashy Spinach Bake

A nicely Italian dish! You could use whatever cheese you like, or you could use tofu.

Ingredients:
1 cup spaghetti squash
1/2 cup butternut squash
1/4 cup cooked spinach
1/4 cup tomato sauce
1/4 tsp thyme
1/4 tsp oregano
2 basil leaves or 1/2 tsp
Salt
Pepper

Directions:
Mix the tomato sauce and spices and set aside. In a small baking dish, layer the spaghetti squash and butternut squash. The last layer should be the spinach. Pour the tomato sauce evenly over the top. If desired, add some cheese as well. Bake at 350 degrees for 30 minutes.

Butternut Strata

Sometimes something I cook turns out so tasty that it's hard for me not to then eat it every night! This is one of those dishes.

Ingredients:
1 cup cubed squash
I slice of polenta (or bread) in chunks
1 egg
Salt to taste

Directions:
Mix well and pour into a small baking dish or a couple of ramekins. I use two small glass bowls. Bake in the oven at 375 for 20 minutes or until the egg is cooked.

Butternut Pizza

Created by me, no alteration necessary! I'm quite pleased with the result! Very, very yummy!

Ingredients:
1 crust dough

1/2 cup butternut squash puréed
1/4 cup sliced tomato
1/4 sliced mushroom
1 oz sliced firm tofu

Directions:
Roll out the dough in a circle on parchment paper. Spread squash purée on the crust. Top with tomato, mushroom, and tofu. Bake at 400 degrees for 20 minutes or until crust is golden brown.

Taquito

One could make this with a variety of vegetables, but this is a great combination!

Ingredients:
1/4 cup corn
1/4 cup chopped carrot
1/4 cup fresh spinach
1/2 cup chopped zucchini
1/2 tsp cumin
1/2 tsp paprika
Tortilla

Directions:
Mix ingredients and spoon into tortilla. Wrap and place tortilla seam side down in a baking dish. Bake at 425 degrees for 13 minutes.

Spinach Enchilada

I didn't add any cumin or paprika to this because I did not want the flavors of the vegetables to be covered. However, for a more Mexican flavored dish, add them both...and a touch of cayenne!

Ingredients:
1/2 cup chopped spinach
1oz firm tofu
1/4 cup white beans
1/4 tsp lime juice
1/4 cup diced tomato
1/4 cup tomato sauce
Tortilla
Cheese

Directions:
Mix spinach, tofu, beans, and lime juice. Add salt. Place in the middle of tortilla, as much as will fit. Roll and place in baking dish with seam at the bottom. Distribute tomatoes and sauce around the tortilla. Top with cheese. Bake at 375 degrees for 20 minutes.

Mini Quiche

A crust-less, simple quiche for a night where you want a hot, but quick dinner. I use small, glass bowls, but a larger Pyrex bowl or oven safe container would work, too.

Ingredients:
1/2 cup chopped spinach
1/4 cup diced tomato
1/4 cup chopped mushroom
1 egg

Directions:
Mix all ingredients thoroughly. Pour into two small glass bowls. Cook at 400 degrees for 15 minutes or until there's browning on the top of each.

Mushroom, Parsnip, Tomato Galette

I do like mushrooms and tomatoes together. The parsnips add an interesting bit to this dish.

Ingredients:
Crust dough_

1/2 cup chopped mushroom
1/2 cup chopped parsnip
1/2 cup diced tomato
Salt
Pepper

Directions:
Press or roll out dough in a circle on parchment paper on a baking sheet. Place all ingredients in the center. Press up the sides, leaving an opening at the top. Bake at 400 degrees for 20 minutes or until crust is browned.

Scalloped Corn

Simple to prepare, fun to eat!

Ingredients:
1/2 cup sliced tomato
1/2 cup corn
1 oz firm tofu
1/4 cup cooked quinoa

Directions:
Layer tomato and corn in a small baking dish. Last layer should be sliced tofu. Sprinkle quinoa on top. Bake in a 350 degree oven for 20 minutes.

Vegetable Kugel

The preparation of this takes no time at all, but be aware that the cook time is 45 minutes and it needs every bit of it! Well worth the time, though.

Ingredients:

1/2 cup chopped mushroom
1/4 cup shredded greens
1/4 cup cooked spinach
1/4 cup diced carrots
1/4 cup diced tomato
1 egg
1/4 cup yogurt
1Tbsp Nutritional yeast
1/2 tsp paprika
1 tsp parsley
Salt
Pepper

Direction:
Mix ingredients and pour into a baking dish. Bake at 375 degrees for 45 minutes.

Black Bean and Yam Enchilada

I didn't use any spices other than salt in order to let the flavors of the ingredients come through. You could add whatever you would like, but I suggest it this way!

Ingredients:
1/2 cup cubed roasted yam
1/2 cup cooked black beans
1/2 cup diced tomato
Tortilla

Directions:
Roast the cubed yam in a 400 degree oven for 20 minutes. Combine with black beans and tomato and roll in the tortilla. Put the tortilla seam down in a baking dish, surround with remaining mixture. Bake at 350 degrees for 20 minutes.

Eggplant and Tofu Bake

One word...delicious. Preparation was simple and the result is scrumptious!

Ingredients:
1 cup eggplant, approx. 4 slices
2Tbsp nutritional yeast
1oz. Firm tofu
1/2 cup tomato diced
1/2 tsp basil
1 tsp parsley
Salt
Pepper
Cheese to top

Directions:
Broil eggplant slices 5 minutes each side.
Mix nutritional yeast, tofu, seasonings, and enough water to make a paste. Layer the eggplant, paste, tomato in a baking dish and top with cheese and s dusting of seasoning. Bake at 350 degrees for 30 minutes.

Navy Bean Bruschetta

This is a combination of several recipes to form something tasty and new. I took a picture on the broiler pan and one on the plate. I served mine with a side of salad and it was a great meal!

Ingredients:

1/4 cup beans
1oz tofu
1/4 cup spinach
1/2 cup diced tomato
1/4 cup corn
1/4 tsp thyme
1/4 tsp oregano
Salt
Grilled bread

Directions:

Blend the beans and tofu until smooth and add spices. Heat. Combine remaining ingredients and heat. Spread bean mixture on the bread and then spread the tomato mixture on top. Put the bruschetta back in the oven to broil another 2 minutes.

Spinach Artichoke Pizza

This pizza uses slices of tomato instead of sauce. I did top mine with a fried egg after it was cooked for protein. My grocery doesn't have fresh artichoke, so I did use canned.

Ingredients:

Crust of choice (basic dough recipe or baked tortilla)

1/4 cup spinach
1/4 cup sliced tomato
1/4 cup sliced mushroom
1/2 cup artichokes
Cheese

Directions:

Layer ingredients on the crust and bake at 400 degrees for 30 minutes, or until crust crisps.

Veggie Balls

I served these over quinoa and tofu, but they would be good over any type of pasta. I think they would be tastier served in a tomato sauce, which I will try next time.

Ingredients:

1/2 cup cooked split peas
1/4 cup chopped carrot
1/4 cup chopped celery
1/4 cup chopped mushroom
1/4 cup chopped tomato
1/4 tsp thyme
1/4 tsp sage
1/4 tsp oil
Parsley
Salt

Directions:

All ingredients go in the food processor or blender. Whir until smooth. Form spoonfuls into balls and place on a parchment paper lined baking sheet. Bake at 400 degrees for 20 minutes. If you choose to make larger sizes or smaller sizes, adjust the baking time! You want these to bounce back a bit to your touch, otherwise they are a bit dry.

Gyro Pizza

One doesn't need cucumbers or lamb to make a great gyro pizza! This surprised me in it's yum factor as it's a "fly by the seat of my pants" recipe!

Ingredients:

1/4 cup seitan, grilled (I flavored my seitan with rosemary and marjoram)
1/2 cup chopped spinach
1/4 cup chopped tomato
1 oz tofu
Dill (I used dehydrated from a summer garden)
1/4 tsp marjoram
1/4 tsp rosemary
Salt
Crust of choice. I use a baked tortilla

Directions:

 Mix 1oz tofu, a bit of water, and dill to taste into a sauce (this is your cucumber sauce without cucumbers).

Mix the spinach with salt, rosemary, and marjoram. Heat. Layer the tomato on the crust. Then, the spinach. Maybe add some mushrooms and/or cheese. Add the dill sauce. Top with the grilled seitan.
Serve it up!

Butternut Squash Galette

Similar to the earlier galette, but with squash and peas!

Ingredients:

Pizza dough
1/4 flour
3Tbsp water
Drop honey
1/2 tsp yeast

Filling
1/2 cup cooked butternut squash
1/2 cup peas
1/2 tsp oil of choice
Salt
Pepper

Directions:

Mix 1Tbsp water, yeast, honey. Add flour and enough water to make dough. Knead. Let rest
15 minutes. Roll or press out into circle. Add the veggies to the center. Press up the edges.
Bake in 400 degree oven until golden. About 25 minutes.

Baked Fried Rice

It's hard to see the rice in my picture, perhaps that's because of the brown table and the brown rice! This is another recipe with a long cook time, so be prepared for it.

Ingredients:

1/2 cup corn
1/2 cup peas
1/4 cup carrots chopped
1/4 cup celery chopped
1/4 cup zucchini chopped
1/2 cup mushrooms chopped
1/4 rice
1/2 tsp oil
Salt
Pepper

Directions:

Preheat oven to 325. Mix ingredients and toss on baking sheet. Bake for 45 to 60 minutes, stirring every 20 minutes. It's done when the rice has a bit of crisp.

Roasted Zucchini and Black Bean Enchilada

This will take a bit of preparation time, so don't plan it on a busy night.

Super yummy, though! Worth every minute!

Ingredients:

1 cup chopped zucchini
1/2 cup black beans
1/4 cup tomato sauce
Cheese
Tortilla
1/2 tsp cumin
1/2 tsp paprika
Salt
Pepper

Directions:

 Preheat oven to 425 degrees. Toss zucchini in cumin, paprika, salt, pepper, and a 1/2 tsp oil. Spray baking sheet. Bake zucchini for 30 minutes, tossing several times. Reduce heat to 375 degrees. Mix beans and zucchini and roll in tortilla with cheese. Place the tortilla in a baking dish with tomato sauce. Brush the tortilla with a bit of oil. Bake for 20 minutes.

Spaghetti Squash Bake

Winter. Lots of squash. Lots of root vegetables. While certainly good, I'm looking forward to summer veggies!

This was a little like lasagna, though not certainly not in texture.

Ingredients:

1 cup spaghetti squash
1/4 cup mushrooms chopped
1/4 cup tomatoes chopped
1/4 cup cooked quinoa
1/4 seitan
Cheese for topping (I used mozzarella)
Salt and pepper

Directions:

Preheat oven to 400 degrees. Layer ingredients in an oiled baking dish. Bake for 30 minutes. Serve!

Eggplant and Spinach "Meat" Balls

These do not need to be spiced, but they can be spiced however you choose. I actually added sage and rosemary to mine with the salt and pepper! Be aware, the prep doesn't take much time, but they do take a while to bake. You could serve this over pasta, rice, quinoa, or spaghetti squash. I ate mine served over spaghetti squash with a side of toasted tofu.

Ingredients:

1/2 cup chopped spinach
1/2 cup eggplant
1/4 cup quinoa
1 Tbsp sunflower seeds

Directions:

Preheat the oven to 350 degrees. Put all the ingredients and your chosen spices into a food processor or blender and whir smooth. Form into walnut sized balls (walnuts with the shells still on) and place them on a parchment paper lined baking sheet. Bake for 30 minutes.

Corn Zucchini Galette

To preface, my pastry is not a true galette pastry. However, staying with my objective of simple, the pastry I used was quick and easy and tasted really good!

Ingredients:

Pizza dough:
1/4 flour
3Tbsp water
Drop honey
1/2 tsp yeast

Filling:
1/2 cup corn
1/2 cup zucchini
Salt
Pepper

Directions:

Sautée zucchini and mix with the corn.

Mix 1Tbsp water, yeast, honey. Add flour and enough water to make dough. Knead. Let rest 15 minutes. Roll or press out into circle. Add the veggies to the center. Press up the edges. Bake in 400 degree oven until golden. About 25 minutes.

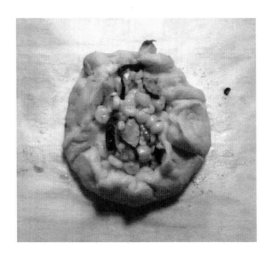

Cauliflower Crust Pizza

I know most of you have heard of this gluten free wonder, but I've changed the recipe to make just one crust! Though, I've made more and froze them for future use, too.

Ingredients:

3/4 cup cooked cauliflower whirred in a food processor (or riced)
1 egg
1oz. firm tofu (if desired for protein)
Mozzarella
Oregano, thyme, salt, pepper to taste

Various toppings (I used spinach, tomato, and mushroom)

Directions:

Preheat oven to 425 degrees. Line a small baking sheet with parchment paper. Mix the ingredients (except for your topping choices). Make a patty. Place in the oven for 20 minutes or until lightly browned. Add toppings. Cook another 10 minutes.

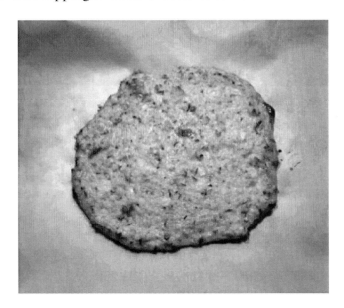

Grilled Eggplant Bake

This takes a little prep time and a bake time, so you'll want to plan it for the right evening! You could experiment with spices, but I wanted to experience the flavors of the veggies.

Ingredients:

1/2 cup eggplant chunked
1/2 cup sliced celery
1/2 cup sliced carrots
1/2 cup chunked tomato
2Tbsp cooked quinoa
1/2 tsp fat of choice
1 Tbsp tomato sauce
Salt
Pepper

Directions:

Preheat oven to 350 degrees. Oil or spray a baking dish.
Pan fry eggplant, carrots, celery. Mix thoroughly with other ingredients.
Put the mixture in the baking dish and bake for 30 minutes.

Roasted Vegetables Part Two

I just can't help it, this winter has been all about the filling root vegetables. The roasting scent in the kitchen and the comforting flavor of the just tender vegetables is just a pleasant way to end the cold days. Plus, the colors bring some light into the shorter days. Again, all these ingredients should be readily obtainable at your grocery store. Remember, that's the point of this blog - seasonal, obtainable, simple, and creative!

No more words, straight to the recipe!

Ingredients:

1/3 cup cubed yam
1/3 cup cubed carrot
1/3 cup cubed parsnip
1/3 cup cubed rutabaga
1/3 cup cubed mushroom
1/3 cup cubed zucchini
1/4 tsp marjoram
1/4 tsp rosemary
1/4 tsp sage
Salt to taste
1/2 tsp fat of choice

Directions:

Preheat the oven to 350 degrees. Spray a baking sheet with non-stick spray or grease with butter. Put your veggies in a bowl and mix them up with the fat of choice and the spices. Mix it up well. The veggies now go in a single layer on the baking sheet. Roast in the oven for approximately 20 minutes or until the vegetables reach your desired tenderness. Serve!

Winter Yum

I cook from scratch, so this will take a little work to do. I create a menu for the week, so I know in advance the nights a dish will take a bit longer. This dish requires chopping, then oven time.

Ingredients:
1/2 cup chopped zucchini
1/2 cup thin sliced parsnip
1/2 cup chunked squash (butternut, delicata, or pumpkin)
1/4 cup chunked mushroom
1/4 chunked tomato
1/4 seitan
Cheese
 1/4 tsp. paprika, sage, pepper.
Salt to taste.

Directions:
Preheat oven to 350 degrees. Spray the inside of a baking dish with no stick spray or coat lightly with olive oil/butter. Toss the veggies in haphazardly. Top with whatever cheese you like in whatever amount. I use 1/2 a stick of string cheese...stringed.

Bake for 20 minutes and serve!

Stovetop

Paprika Tofu

Interesting smoky flavor.

Ingredients:
1 cup spaghetti squash
1/2 cup diced tomato
1 ounce firm tofu, cubed
1 tsp paprika
1Tbsp water

Directions:
Earlier in the day, set the tofu to marinate in the paprika and water. Put it in a dish that ensures the tofu is covered by the marinade and place it in the refrigerator. When you are ready to prepare the meal, pour the marinade and tofu into a small skillet with the tomatoes and sautee until heated through, some liquid should remain. Heat the spaghetti squash in the microwave until its warm, about 2 minutes. Pour the tofu sauce over the spaghetti squash and serve.

Ropa Vieja

Feel free to add the red and green peppers and onions to this dish, I realize some people aren't sensitive to them. But, in my opinion, this was quite good without them!

Ingredients:
1/4 cup seitan cut in strips
1/2 cup diced tomato
1/4 tsp cumin
1/4 tsp oregano
1/4 tsp turmeric
dash cayenne
dash cinnamon
1/2 cup water

Directions:
Place all ingredients in a small saucepan. Bring to a boil, then reduce heat to simmer and cover.
Simmer for 30 minutes. Serve over rice.

Fajita

This was easy to make! Now, you could add the green peppers and onions if you are not sensitive to them.

Ingredients:
1/4 cup seitan
1/4 tsp cumin
1/4 tsp paprika
dash cayenne pepper
1 ounce firm tofu
1 Tbsp yogurt
1/4 cup diced tomato

Tortilla, pita, or thin pancake

Directions:
Sautee the seitan with the spices until it's just shy of crispy. Mix the yogurt and tofu to make a thick sauce. The seitan will go on the tortilla/pita/thin pancake. Add the tofu sauce and top with the tomato.

Spaghetti Squash with Dill, Tomato, and Mushroom

A great combination. If you wanted, you could make some regular noodles to mix in with the squash.

Ingredients:
1 cup cooked spaghetti squash
2 Tbsp fresh dill or 1 tsp dried dill
1/2 cup diced mushroom
1/2 cup diced tomato
Salt to taste

Directions:
Sautee the tomato and mushroom with the dill until the mushroom is soft. Mix with the spaghetti squash and microwave until heated through, about 2 minutes.

Pizza 'Dillas

Pizza in a quesadilla! I sauteed my veggies first, but you don't need to.

Ingredients:
1 corn or flour tortilla
1/4 cup tomato sauce
1/4 cup diced tomato
1/4 cup mushroom
Cheese of choice to taste
Dash oregano
Dash thyme
Salt to taste

Directions:
Mix all the ingredients and spoon on half the tortilla. Top with the other half and cook in a lightly greased skillet until each side is golden brown.

Corn and Black Bean Quesadilla

The radishes give this a nice bite and a unique crunch.

Ingredients:
1/2 cup corn
1/2 cup chopped radish
1/2 cup cooked black beans, pureed
1/4 tsp cumin
1/4 tsp paprika
Tortilla

Directions:
Mix the ingredients, except the tortilla, and heat. Cut the tortilla in half and spread the mix on one half. Top with the other half and pan sear until the tortilla is crispy.

Spaghetti Squash and Peas

Nothing wrong with a good combination of vegetables!

Ingredients:
1 cup cooked spaghetti squash
1/2 cup peas
1/2 cup diced eggplant
1 ounce firm tofu, cubed

Directions:
Sautee the eggplant, peas, and tofu with a bit of oil.   Mix with the squash and heat in the microwave until hot, approximately 2 minutes. Serve with salt and pepper to taste.

Grits and Sauteed Vegetables

So easy and so delicious!

Ingredients:
1 pkg grits, prepared (1/2 cup)
1/2 cup sliced and quartered zucchini
1/2 cup sliced mushroom
1/2 cup tomato
1/2 cup shredded cabbage
1 ounce firm tofu, cubed

Directions:
Sautee the veggies until tender. Mix with the grits and serve!

Tsars Revenge

This tasted great. However, the smoke alarm dismantled on the counter tales the true tale.

Ingredients:
1 cup cabbage
1/2 cup potato
1 ounce firm tofu
1/4 tsp paprika
1/4 tsp vinegar
salt to taste
veggie broth

Directions:
Slice the cabbage and shred into smallish pieces. Cut the potato in medium squares. Slice the tofu into cubes. Sautee with a bit of oil in a skillet until the ingredients are burnt (yes, burnt) to the bottom. Add the paprika and salt and stir. Then, add just enough broth to cover the ingredients and boil briefly, while stirring. Be sure to get as much of the burnt ingredients incorporated as possible. Add the vinegar. If you feel you want a bit more bite, add more vinegar.

Parsnip Cakes

Sort of like potato pancakes, but with parsnips.

Ingredients:
1/2 cup sliced parsnips
1 egg
1/4 cup quinoa
salt to taste

Directions:
Boil the parsnips until they are tender. Drain. Mash the parsnips in a mixing bowl and add the egg, quinoa, and salt. Mix thoroughly. Spoon in pancake sized portions onto a skillet and cook until golden brown on both sides.

Boxty

Potatoes in a pancake, nothing wrong with that!

Ingredients:
1/2 cup mashed potato
1/4 cup grated sweet potato
1/4 cup flour
1/2 tsp baking soda
1 egg
salt

Directions:
Mix all the ingredients together in a small bowl. Spoon pancake sized portions onto a skillet and cook until golden brown on both sides.

Ginger Cardamom Carrots

Wow! Just enough ginger to give it a kick and that cardamom gives it a nice balance.

Ingredients:
1 cup sliced carrots
1/4 tsp ginger
1/4 tsp cardamom
1/4 tsp paprika
Salt
Tofu

Directions:
Sautee all ingredients in a skillet with a bit of oil until the carrots are tender.

Curried Veggie Pasties

These tasted really yummy, but looked not so great. I think it will take some practice!

Ingredients:
1/4 cup diced potato
1/4 cup diced sweet potato
1 ounce firm tofu, cubed
1/2 cup peas
1/4 cup diced carrot
1/4 cup flour
1/2 tsp curry
1/4 tsp cumin

Directions:
Heat the potatoes in a covered skillet until tender. Add the carrot and heat for an additional 3-5 minutes, covered. Remove from heat and add peas and spices. Mix and stir in half the flour. Wet hands and roll into equal sized small patties. Coat with the remaining flour (dredge them) and pan fry on both sides until golden brown.

Sauteed Spinach and Mushroom

You'll want to sautee this until the spinach has lost about half of its liquid.

Ingredients:
1/2 cup cooked spinach
1/2 cup diced mushroom
1 ounce firm tofu, cubed
1/4 cup diced tomato

Directions:
Sautee the ingredients in a skillet, salt to taste, and serve over noodles, rice, or quinoa.

Italian Eggs

So easy and so good!

Ingredients:
1/2 cup tomato sauce
1/2 cup chopped spinach
1/4 tsp thyme
1 egg

Directions:

Mix the tomato sauce, spinach, and thyme. Pour into a small skillet and heat on medium until the sauce bubbles. Crack the egg into the center and cover the skillet. Continue to cook for 3-5 minutes. Serve!

Zucchini Balls

A little finicky, making sure each side of the ball is browned, but well worth the effort.

Ingredients:
3/4 cup grated zucchini
1/4 tsp basil
1 ounce firm tofu
Salt
Bit of cornmeal

Directions:
Squish as much liquid as you can out of the grated zucchini. Mix in the basil and the tofu. Add just enough cornmeal to make small balls that hold together. Place each ball in a skillet and pan fry until golden brown on each side.

Use these on spaghetti or spaghetti squash with a bit of tomato sauce.

Squash, Corn, Barley Succotash

I used a sauce pan for this delicious dinner.

Ingredients:
1/4 cup cooked barley
1 cup squash (acorn, butternut, pumpkin, delicata) cubed
1/2 cup corn
1/4 cup water
Salt
Pepper
1/4 tsp thyme

Directions:
Simmer the squash and thyme with the water in a covered pan until the squash is tender, 10-15 minutes. Add the corn and re-cover to simmer for 5 minutes more. Add the barley and heat through. Serve.

Corn, Tomato, Kale Mixer

Any meal that goes entirely in the skillet is a good one!

Ingredients:
1 cup kale
1/2 cup corn
1/2 cup diced tomato
1/2 cup cooked black beans
1/4 tsp cumin
1/4 tsp paprika

Directions:
Put all ingredients in a skillet with a bit of oil and salt and pepper to taste. Sautee until heated through and the kale is wilted.

Beans and Greens

I used kale and arugula in this dish and it was amazing!

Ingredients:
1/2 cup cooked white beans
1 cup greens of choice (kale, spinach)
1/2 tsp apple cider vinegar
Salt
Pepper
Croutons

Directions:
Make your own croutons by cubing the bread you wish to use and baking it in the oven on a baking sheet at 400 degrees for 10 minutes.

Sautée the beans with the apple cider vinegary until heated through. Remove and set aside. Sautée the greens with salt and pepper and a bit of oil until they are wilted. Mix with beans and top with croutons.

Vegetarian Quiella

This is a spin on paella. In this area, there are simply no saffron noodles to be found....anywhere! I created this instead!

Ingredients:
1/2 cup spaghetti squash
1/4 cup diced zucchini
1/4 cup diced carrots
1/4 cup peas
1/4 cup diced yellow squash
1/4 cup cubed and peeled eggplant
1/4 cup diced tomato
1 ounce firm tofu cubed
1/4 cup quinoa
1/2 tsp paprika
1 bay leaf
3 sprigs parsley
1/4 cup veggie broth

Directions:
Sautée everything except the quinoa, broth, and parsley in a bit of oil for 5 minutes. Add the broth and quinoa and simmer until the mixture is thickened. Remove the bay leaf and add the parsley. Serve.

Eggplant Wrap

Quick and filling meal to prepare after a long day!

Ingredients:
1/2 cup cubed and peeled eggplant
1 ounce firm tofu, cubed
1/2 cup diced tomato
1/4 tsp basil
1/ tsp thyme
Tortilla

Directions:
Sautée veggies and spices until the eggplant is tender. Spoon into a tortilla, roll it up, and serve!

Egg in Tomato Sauce

I cannot believe how yummy this is for how simple the cooking is!

Ingredients:
1/2 cup tomato sauce
1 egg

Directions:
Heat the sauce until warm through. Crack the egg into the sauce. Cover and cook for 5 minutes. Uncover, remove from heat, and let stand for 2 - 3 minutes. Serve over toasted bread.

Lima Bean Sweet Potato Toast

A quickly prepared and quite tasty dinner.

Ingredients:
1/2 cup cooked Lima beans
1/4 cup cooked diced sweet potato
1/4 cup avocado
1 ounce firm tofu
1/4 cup diced zucchini
1/4 cup corn
1 piece toasted bread

Directions:
Put Lima beans, sweet potato, avocado, and tofu in a food processor or blender and purée.
Spread the mixture in the toast, salt to taste. Heat the corn and zucchini and spoon on top of the
toast. Serve.

Eggplant Sketti with Beans

The pinto beans provide a nice additional texture to this dish.

Ingredients:
1 cup cooked spaghetti squash
1/2 cup cubed eggplant
1/2 cup diced tomato
1/2 cup cooked pinto beans

Directions:
Sautée the eggplant and tomato together until the eggplant is tender. Use a bit of your oil of choice. Add the mixture to the spaghetti squash. Add the beans. Mix well and heat in the microwave about 1 minute, make sure it's heated through. Serve!

Make sure you peel your eggplant for this, you want it nice and tender!

Ingredients:
1/2 cup sliced, peeled eggplant
1/2 cup sliced zucchini
1/4 cup diced red bell pepper
1/4 cup diced mushroom
1/4 cup diced tomato
Bread vehicle of choice

For "mayo:"
1 ounce firm tofu
1/4 tsp lemon juice
1/2 tsp oil of choice

Directions:
Mix the tofu, lemon juice, oil, and salt to taste with enough water to make a spread of mayo-like consistency. Set aside.

Sautée the veggies with salt and pepper to taste until they are tender.

Spread the "mayo" on your bread of choice. Top with your sautéed vegetables. Serve!

Biscuit and Gravy

Quite simple and much more healthy than other versions!

Ingredients:
Biscuit:
1/8 cup cornmeal
1/8 cup flour
1/2 tsp baking powder
1/4 tsp baking soda
Enough water for thick dough

Gravy:
1 ounce firm tofu
Water to make gravy consistency
Black pepper
Salt

Directions:
For the biscuit:
Mix the ingredients and let sit for 5 minutes. Spoon into a skillet and cook until each side is golden brown.

For the gravy:
Mix all ingredients until a consistency you prefer is achieved.

Heat the "gravy" and pour over the biscuit.

Eggplant Philly Sandwich

Eggplant can absorb the flavor of just about anything and this easy sandwich is super yummy!

Ingredients:
1/2 cup sliced eggplant
1/2 cup sliced mushroom
1/2 cup sliced zucchini
1/2 cup sliced tomato
1 ounce firm tofu
Black pepper
Salt
Cheese
Pita, hoagie roll, thin pancake, tortilla

Directions:
Sautée the vegetables, tofu, and spices until the veggies are tender. Spoon onto the bread vehicle of choice. Top with the cheese. Eat!

Summer Vegetable Skillet Enchilada

The arugula adds a special flavor to this, but if you don't have it, try leaf spinach or kale.

Ingredients:
1/2 cup diced zucchini
1/2 cup corn
1/2 cup diced tomato
1/4 cup diced summer squash
1/4 cup arugula
1/2 cup cooked beans
1/4 tsp cumin
1/4 tsp paprika
Salt
1/4 cup water or veggie broth

Directions:
Put all ingredients except beans and arugula into a skillet and simmer until tender. Add the beans and arugula and heat until the arugula is wilted. Top with tortilla strips and serve.

Zucchini Noodles and Fried Egg

Have a busy day and want an easy meal? This is it! I use my carrot peeler for zucchini noodles!

Ingredients:
1 cup zucchini noodles
1 egg
1 ounce firm tofu

Directions:
Fry the egg to your preference. Mix the zucchini noodles and tofu, heat in the microwave until warmed. Top with the egg and serve.

Note: This can be made with spaghetti squash as well.

Tuscan Skillet Seitan

This was very, very good! I might cut the seitan up smaller when I cook it again.

Ingredients:
1/4 cup seitan cut in rounds
1/2 cup sliced mushrooms
1/2 cup diced tomato
1/4 cup tomato sauce
1/2 cup cooked white beans
1 tsp lemon juice
1/4 tsp oregano
1/4 tsp thyme
4 leaves of basil

Directions:
Place all ingredients in a skillet and cook on medium heat for 10-15 minutes or until the tomato sauce has mostly been absorbed.

Spinach Mushroom Quesadilla

Extremely easy to throw together. Tasty with button mushrooms, but I used baby bellas (on sale at the grocery) and WOW!

Ingredients:
1/2 cup cooked spinach
1/2 cup sliced mushrooms
Tortilla

Directions:
Sautée the spinach and mushrooms I'm a skillet with a bit of oil until heated through. Put the mixture on half the tortilla. Top with the other half. Cook in the skillet until lightly browned on each side.

Nacho Pizza

Can't go wrong with this one!

Ingredients:
Tortilla
1/2 cup refried beans
1/4 cup diced tomato
1/4 diced red pepper
1/4 cup taco spiced seitan
1/4 cup shredded lettuce

Directions:
Bake the tortilla until it is crisp. I do this in a skillet. Heat the refried beans and the taco seitan.
Spread the beans on the tortilla. Add the seitan, then the tomato, pepper, and top with the lettuce.
Serve!

Charred Corn and Tofu Toast

I suggest making this with fresh sweet corn! It is SO GOOD! Also, a nice meal for a summer evening, simple with little to warm up the kitchen.

Ingredients:
Bread
1 cup corn
1/4 cup avocado
1 tsp lemon juice
Salt
1 ounce firm tofu, sliced

Directions:
Toast the bread. Lightly char/blacken the corn in a skillet. Purée the avocado with lemon juice and salt to taste.
Spread the avocado on the toast. Place the tofu on next. Then, spoon the corn on top of that. Serve!

Tailgate Three Bean Italiano

So much fresh vegetable goodness in this dish. Earlier I introduced you to Tailgate Three Bean. This adds some ingredients and takes away some others to make it "Italiano."

Ingredients:
1/4 cup cooked black beans
1/4 cup cooked white beans
1/2 cup green beans
1/4 cup corn
1/4 cup sliced celery
1/4 tomato sauce
1/4 tsp oregano
3 basil leaves
Salt
Pepper
1tsp Nutritional Yeast (optional)

Directions:
Mix all ingredients together in a skillet and sautée until the green beans are tender, about ten minutes.

Kale and Artichoke Quesadilla

What a tasty combination! Wilted kale is really yummy!

Ingredients:
1 cup kale
1/2 cup artichoke hearts
1/4 cup diced mushroom
Tortilla

Directions:
Sautée the kale, mushroom, and artichoke together in a bit of oil until the kale is wilted. Salt and pepper to taste. Put the mixture on half the tortilla and top with the other half. Pan sear until lightly browned on both sides.

Sweet Potato Corn Cake

I cooked my sweet potato in the microwave and mashed with a fork. However, you could use a food processor. This dish was outstandingly good!

Ingredients:
1/2 cup sweet potato purée
1 egg
1/2 cup corn
1/4 cup cornmeal

Directions:
Mix all ingredient. Spoon the mixture into a skillet and cook until lightly browned on each side.

Spinach Pancake

I'm all about tossing things together and putting them in a skillet!

Ingredients:
1/2 cup chopped spinach
1/4 cup flour
1 egg
1/4 teaspoon baking powder
Pinch baking soda
Salt

Directions:
Mix ingredients together and cook in a skillet until lightly browned on both sides.

S.O.S.

Most people know this as Dried Beef Gravy. I remember it from childhood as a quick and easy dish that was delicious. So, I decided I would try to manipulate it into a vegetarian dish. I've also made it low fat!

Ingredients:
1 ounce firm tofu
1/4 cup sliced seitan
Toasted bread
Salt
Pepper

Directions:
Mix the tofu with enough water to make gravy. Salt and pepper to taste. Pan fry seitan with salt and pepper and a bit of oil. Put seitan on toast and top with tofu gravy. Serve.

Shakshuka

A different dish to try in the summer time when you don't want to heat up the kitchen. Quite good!

Ingredients:
1/4 cup diced tomato
1/4 cup diced red pepper
1/4 cup diced mushroom
3/4 cup tomato sauce
1 egg
1/4 cup cooked white beans
1/4 tsp cumin
1/4 tsp paprika
1/4 tsp turmeric
Salt
Pepper
Pinch of basil

Directions:
Sautée the red pepper, tomato, and spices with a bit of oil in a small sauce pan until the pepper is tender. Add the tomato sauce, mushroom, and beans. Mix well. Crack the egg into the center. Cover and simmer until the egg white is firm, 8-10 minutes.

Fiesta Fry Pan

A great combination of veggies!

Ingredients:
1/2 cup diced yellow squash
1/2 cup diced tomato
1/2 cup corn
1/2 cup cooked pinto beans
1/4 cup cooked quinoa
1/4 tsp cumin
1/4 tsp paprika
Salt

Directions:
Place all ingredients in a skillet and sautée with a bit of oil. When the squash is tender, remove from heat. Plate and serve!

Spinach and Tomato Quesadilla

I cannot wait for garden fresh tomatoes for this recipe!

Ingredients:
1/2 cup chopped spinach
1/2 cup diced tomato
Tortilla
Salt
Pepper

Directions:
Mix the spinach and tomato and spice to your taste.   Warm in the microwave about 1 minute.
Spread on the tortilla and sear on each side until lightly browned.

Avocado Pizza

There are so many ways to create a pizza without tomato sauce. This one is especially good!

Ingredients:
1/4 avocado
1 ounce tofu
Tortilla

Directions:
Mix the tofu and avocado into a thick sauce using a bit of water. Bake the tortilla so it's crisp. Spread the sauce on the tortilla and top with veggies of your choice.

Thai Fried Quinoa

I don't like my food really spicy, especially in hot weather. Feel free to add more curry to this if you want a little more fire!

Ingredients:
1/4 cup cooked quinoa
1 cup green beans
1/4 cup chopped red pepper
1 ounce firm tofu cubed
1/4 tsp curry powder
Pinch of ginger powder
Salt

Directions:
Mix all ingredients and sautée with a bit of oil until beans are just tender.

Philly Mushroom Sandwich

This was incredibly tasty!

Ingredients:
1/2 cup sliced mushrooms
1 ounce firm tofu, sliced
Mozzarella cheese
Salt
Pepper
Bread of choice (I made a thin pancake)

Directions:
Sautée the mushrooms with salt, pepper, and a little oil. Place them on the bread, top with tofu slices and cheese.

Black Bean Taco Salad

I enjoy the flavor of black beans, corn, and tomato without spices. However, for a more Mexican flair, add cumin and paprika.

Ingredients:
1/2 cup cooked black beans
1/2 cup corn
1/2 cup diced tomato
Salt
Pepper
Cumin and paprika (optional)
Tortilla

Directions:
Sautée the ingredients except the tortilla. Cut the tortilla into strips and bake. Server the warm mixture over greens and top with the tortilla.

Yellow Squash Fritter

Yellow squash is also known as summer squash and Crookneck squash. No matter the name, it makes these super tasty.

Ingredients:
1 cup diced yellow squash
1 egg
1/4 cup cooked quinoa
Salt
Pepper

Directions:
Mix the ingredients and pan fry until each side is lightly browned.

Skillet Enchilada

A great way to have an enchilada without heating the kitchen up in the summer.

Ingredients:
1/2 cup black beans
1/2 cup corn
1/2 cup tomato
Tortilla
1/4 tsp cumin
1/4 tsp paprika
Salt

Directions:
Cut the tortilla into bite sized pieces and bake in a skillet until crispy. Remove and set aside.
Mix the rest of the ingredients. Sautée until heated through. Add the tortilla and mix. Serve.

Gyro

Ingredients:
1/4 cup seitan
1/4 tsp marjoram
1/4 tsp Rosemary
1/4 tsp sage
1 oz tofu
1 tsp dill
Pita or thin pancake

Directions:
Sautée the seitan with rosemary, marjoram, and sage. Mix the tofu and fill into a sauce. Put the seitan on the pita and top with dill sauce.

Zucchini Mushroom Roll Up

Zucchini and mushroom sauteed together...delectable!

Ingredients:
1/2 cup diced zucchini
1/2 cup diced mushroom
1oz tofu
Salt
Pepper
Tortilla

Directions:
Sautée the veggies and tofu in the oil of your choice. Spread in the tortilla and roll it up!

Veggie Black Bean Pizza

Ingredients:
1/4 cup chopped zucchini
1/4 cup chopped yellow squash
1/4 cup chopped mushroom
1/4 cup diced tomato
1/2 cup chopped carrot
1/4 cup chopped radish
1/4 cup chopped parsnip
1/2 cup black beans
Salt
Tortilla

Directions:
Bake the tortilla.
Heat the black beans, add about a Tbsp of water and whir smooth in a blender or food processor. Spread on the tortilla.
Sautée the zucchini, yellow squash, tomato, and mushroom with a bit of oil. Mix with the other veggies and put as much as desired on the bean tortilla.

Two Beans and Tofu Tomato

Quick and easy and delicious!

Ingredients:
1/2 cup wax beans
1/2 cup green beans
1/2 cup diced tomato
1oz tofu
1/2 tsp basil
Salt
Pepper

Directions:
Put the ingredients in a pan and sautée until heated through.

Southern Quinoa

This combination is spectacular!

Ingredients:
1/4 cup cooked quinoa
1/4 cup pinto beans
1/2 cup diced tomato
1/2 cup corn
1 Tbsp Rotel
1oz firm tofu

Directions:
Make a thick sauce with the Rotel and tofu. Mix the rest of the ingredients and combine with the sauce. Heat and serve.

Quinoa And Summer Squash

A great dish for summer. Easy to make with just a few ingredients and not over-filling for a hot evening!

Ingredients:
1/2 cup chopped summer squash
1/2 cup diced tomato
1oz firm tofu
2 sprigs parsley
2 leaves basil
1/2 tsp oil
1 tsp red wine vinegar
Salt
Pepper
1/4 cup cooked quinoa

Directions:
Sautée squash, tomatoes, tofu, spices, oil, and vinegar until squad is tender.
Add quinoa and stir until incorporated and warm.

Serve over mixed greens.

Mediterranean Ratatouille

I served this over quinoa, but one could serve it over rice or even over noodles.

Ingredients:
1/2 cup chopped eggplant
1/2 cup chopped summer squash
1/4 cup chopped zucchini
1/4 cup chopped mushroom
1/2 cup diced tomato
1/2 tsp basil
1/4 tsp thyme
1/2 tsp parsley
Salt
1/4 cup veggie broth

Directions:
Put all ingredients in a skillet type pan and sautée until the veggies are tender.

Sauteed Veggie Pizza

This is the season for sauteed vegetables. An excellent way to serve them. I did not add cheese, but you could!

Ingredients:
1/2 cup chopped zucchini
1/2 cup chopped mushroom
1/4 cup kale
1/4 cup diced tomato
1 oz firm tofu
1 tortilla

Directions:
Sautée the vegetables and tofu in a little oil and salt and pepper. Bake the tortilla. Top the tortilla and serve!!

Calabacita Tacos

I recommend these with a little guacamole!

Ingredients:
1/2 cup chopped summer squash
1/2 cup corn
1/2 cup cooked black beans
1/4 tsp cumin
1/4 tsp paprika
Salt to taste
Taco shell

Directions:
Sautée the squash and corn with the spices. Add the beans and heat through.   Fill the taco shell and garnish as desired.

Taco Salad

Quick and easy, great for a summer meal.

Ingredients:
1 cup shredded lettuce
1/2 cup diced tomato
1/4 cup corn
1/4 cup chopped mushroom
1/4 cup cooked black beans
1/4 cup seitan

Baked tortilla

Directions:
Chop the seitan into small chunks and sautée with cumin, paprika, and salt to taste. Heat the beans. Break the tortilla into bite sized chips. Mix all ingredients together.

Spanish Vegetable Casserole

The taste of this is something truly special.

Ingredients:
1/4 cup cubed eggplant
1/2 cup green beans
1/2 cup cubed sweet potato (or potato)
1/2 cup diced tomato
1/4 cup cubed pear
1/2 cup cooked pinto beans
1 tsp paprika
Salt
Pepper

Directions:
Put ingredients in a small saucepan with 1/2 cup water. Bring to a boil, then reduce heat and simmer until the vegetables are tender.

Seared Corn Bruschetta

This could also be done with grilled corn. The searing is easy, just keep an eye on it and stir so it doesn't POP!

Ingredients:
1/2 cup corn
1/2 cup diced tomato
1/4 tsp thyme
Salt to taste
Bread of choice

Directions:
Lightly sear the corn in a skillet. Mix with tomato and thyme. Put the bread (I cut mine in quarters) in the oven on broil for 5 minutes on each side, until toasted. Top with a spoonful of the mixture.   You may want to broil it for another two minutes.

Carrot Fritter

Very interesting flavor. Definitely grate the carrots, don't try to chop them.

Ingredients:
1 cup grated carrot
1 egg
1/4 cup quinoa

Directions:
Combine and add salt to taste. Pan fry on each side until lightly browned.

Green Pea Soup

Really tasty with frozen peas. I can't wait to try it with fresh peas!

Ingredients:
1 cup peas
1/2 cup fresh spinach
3/4 cup water
1 tsp basil
1/2 tsp lemon juice
Salt

Directions:
In a sauce pan, cover the peas with water and boil. Add the spinach, basil, lemon juice, and salt to taste. Heat until spinach is limp. Serve!

Indian Korma

If you want a bit more "bite," increase the ginger to 1/2 tsp. Be sure you simmer and don't boil this, or you'll need to add some water!

Ingredients:
1/2 cup chopped carrot
1/2 cup peas
1/2 cup tomato sauce
1/2 cup diced potato
1 oz tofu
1/4 tsp ginger
1/4 tsp cumin

Directions:
Mix the tofu with enough water to make a thick sauce. Set aside. Put the carrots, potato, tomato sauce, ginger, cumin, and salt to taste in a sauce pan and cook on medium low until the potato is tender. Add peas and tofu sauce and simmer for 10 minutes. Serve with quinoa.

Black Bean and Corn Quesadilla

Quick, easy, and super tasty!

Ingredients:
1/2 cup cooked black beans
1/2 cup corn
1/2 cup diced tomato
Tortilla

Directions:
Heat the beans, corn, and tomato in the microwave.   Spoon a good amount in the tortilla and pan fry.

"Crab" Cakes

Back in the day, before enlightenment, I did enjoy a good crab cake! Remember, Old Bay is spicy hot!

Ingredients:
1 cup grated zucchini
1 egg
1Tsp flour of choice
1/2 tsp Old Bay
Salt

Directions:
Combine ingredients. Spoon portions on to a skillet and pan fry until lightly browned on each side.

Indian Keema

The spices on this were perfect. It was incredibly delicious!!

Ingredients:
1/4 cup seitan
1/2 cup diced tomato
1 cup peas
1 tsp lime juice
1/8 tsp curry
1/8 tsp cumin
1/8 tsp ginger
1/4 tsp cinnamon
1/4 tsp turmeric
1/2 tsp oil

Directions:
Sautée the seitan with oil and spices for 5 minutes. Add tomato and lime and sautée. Then, add peas and sautée until heated through. Serve over quinoa or rice.

Sweet Potato Zucchini Quesadilla

Incredibly good! I chose not to use any spice but salt so I could get the flavor of the sweet potato and zucchini and I'm so pleased!

Ingredients:
1 cup shredded zucchini
1/2 cup cubed cooked sweet potato
Tortilla

Directions:
Mix zucchini and sweet potato and spread on tortilla. Pan sear on each side. Serve with sides of choice!

Zucchini Pancake

When spicing, I would add more pepper than you think you want. The zucchini needs a little "lift."

Ingredients:
1 cup grated zucchini
1 egg
1/2 tsp parsley
Salt
Pepper
Enough flour of choice to make thicken

Directions:
Mix ingredients. Spoon pancake sized portions into a skillet and fry until browned on each side.

Tailgate Three Bean

Quite a nice flavor. If you like a little heat, add more mustard!

Ingredients:
1/4 cup black beans
1/4 cup white beans
1/2 cup green beans
1/4 cup corn
1/4 cup chopped celery
1/4 cup veggie broth
Dash of ground mustard
2 sprigs fresh parsley
Salt
Pepper
1 tsp nutritional yeast

Directions:
Place all ingredients in a saucepan and sautée until tender.

Black Bean, Squash, Corn Mix Up

DELICIOUS!

Ingredients:

1 cup squash (butternut or delicata) cubed
1/4 cup yam diced
1/4 cup tomato diced
1/2 cup cooked black beans
1/2 cup cooked corn
1/4 cup veggie broth
1/4 tsp oregano
1/4tsp cumin
salt

Directions:

Put the squash, yam, tomato, spices, and broth in a sauce pan and cook until tender. Add the black beans and corn and heat through. Serve with tortilla chips or polenta.

Pean Pancakes

Unusual, but easy peasy to prepare and pretty tasty!

Ingredients:
1 cup cooked peas
1 egg
Bit of cornflour to thicken, if necessary
Salt
Pepper

Directions:
All ingredients go in the food processor or blender. Whir until smooth. Don't add too much cornflour because you don't want the pancake to be too dry. Pan fry until lightly browned on each side.

Corn and Black Bean Tacos

Ingredients:

1/2 cup corn
1/2 cup chopped radish
1/2 cup cooked black beans
1/4 slice avocado
1/4 tsp cumin
1/4 tsp paprika
1/2 tsp lime juice
Salt
Corn or flour tortilla

Directions:

Mix the ingredients. Heat. Spread on tortilla with your choice of toppings! I had some avocado, lettuce, and tomato with mine.

Spinach Bean Quesadilla

Quite tasty! You could add more cumin and paprika, even a little cayenne, if you like. Or, you could not use them at all. I had some with just salt and pepper and it was yummy.

Ingredients:

1/2 cup cooked spinach
1/2 cup white beans
1/2 tsp oil
Dash cumin
Dash paprika
Salt
Pepper

Directions:

Place all ingredients in food processor or blender and whir smooth.
Spread on a tortilla and pan grill/fry. Serve with lettuce, tomato, avocado, etc.

Squash Cauliflower Cakes

Very much a pancake made from veggies!

Ingredients:

1/2 cup cooked cauliflower
1/2 cup cooked butternut or delicata squash
1/4 cup quinoa
1 egg
salt
pepper
cinnamon or nutmeg

Directions:

Put the cauliflower, squash, and quinoa in a blender or food processor and whir. Add the egg. Pour in patties on to a skillet and pan fry until lightly brown on each side. I garnished one with nutmeg, one with cinnamon, and one with salt and pepper. Each was quite good! I suggest you follow the same idea!

Egg and Squash Sandwich

This is a quick and simple dinner. I make my squash puree just by cooking the squash, adding a bit of water, and mashing with a fork. Butternut squash or delicata squash work the best for this.

Ingredients:

1/2 cup squash purée
Salt
Egg
Bread (I toasted mine)

Directions:

Toast bread. Spread on purée. Top with fried egg or scrambled egg.

Squash Quesadilla

I made this with butternut squash, but you could use delicata or pumpkin as well! It makes a lot of filling, so you may want to use more than one tortilla!

Ingredients:

1 cup squash purée
1 ounce firm tofu
Cumin (to taste)
Paprika (to taste)
Salt
Pepper
Tortilla (corn or flour)

Directions:

 Mix the tofu, puree, and spices together in a small bowl. Spread in a medium thickness layer on half a tortilla. Cover with the other half. Pan fry in skillet until each side is lightly browned.

Spaghetti Squash Cakes

These are remarkably similar to the Squash/Pumpkin Fritters in the creation, but have a much different taste. Simple, filling, seasonal and very tasty.

Ingredients:

2Tbsp ground quick oats
1 cup spaghetti squash
1 one egg
Cheese of choice (shredded)
Salt
Pepper

Directions:

I ground my quick oats in a coffee grinder. You could also use a food processor. Mix the ingredients together, using just as much cheese as you feel necessary. I only used about 1Tbsp. Make sure everything is incorporated.

Pour into small pancake sized portions on your skillet. Pan fry both sides until lightly browned. I used some cracked pepper on mine before I flipped them. To me, the pepper really compliments the spaghetti squash.

Caulifredo

Ingredients:

1/2 cup cooked white beans
1/2 cup cooked cauliflower
1/4 cup water (more or less depending on how you like your sauce)
1/2tsp olive oil
Salt
Cracked pepper

1 cup spaghetti squash
1/4 cup cooked pasta noodles.

Directions:

Add the white beans, cauliflower, water, olive oil, salt and cracked pepper to taste to a blender or food processor and whir it smooth. If you like your sauce thicker, start with less water and add it until it gets to the consistency you would prefer.

Heat the spaghetti squash and cooked pasta noodles together and add the sauce. I then topped it with more cracked pepper for a bit more "bite."

Mexiplant

Ingredients:
1 cup cubed eggplant
1/2 cup sliced and quartered zucchini
1/2 cup tomato sauce
1 tsp cumin
1/2 tsp paprika
Dusting cayenne
Salt
1 tbsp lime juice
1oz. firm tofu cubed
1 tsp. olive oil

Directions:
Place all ingredients in a sauce pan and simmer for one hour, stirring occasionally. You may need to add more liquid if you accidentally simmer at too high a temperature.

Squash Fritters

You can use squash or pumpkin (you can even use canned pumpkin). I've used delicata squash, butternut squash, canned pumpkin, and fresh pumpkin. I think I like the butternut squash the best, though. An aside - for a single person, a delicata squash is super. It's small enough to provide squash for this and for soup another night.

Ingredients:

1/2 cup squash
1/2 cup corn (fresh, canned, or frozen but now thawed)
1/4 cup quinoa (cooked)
1 egg
salt
pepper
cinnamon (if desired)

Directions:
First, you want to cook your squash choice. You can bake it in the oven and cube it after or you can cube it and nuke it. You want your squash pretty soft, however you choose to do it.

You'll put the squash in a small mixing bowl and squish it up with a fork. I have a limited amount of appliances in my kitchen, but if you have food processor, you could whir it up, but why make something else dirty when a fork will do?

After squishing the squash (giggle) pretty well, a few chunks won't matter, put in your corn, quinoa, and egg. Add salt and pepper to taste. Mix it all up.

Spray a fry pan with non-stick spray or use an oil to lightly coat the pan. You'll spoon the mixture on to the surface in patties of a medium size. I like to then sprinkle each patty with a dash of cinnamon for some extra yum, but it certainly isn't necessary. Cook just as you would a pancake. When the edges look non-glossy, go ahead and flip them. You want to make sure they are pretty well cooked before flipping though, lest they fall apart during the flip. The flip side requires much less cook time.

Made in United States
North Haven, CT
28 October 2022